IMAGES
of Aviation

PACIFIC SOUTHWEST
AIRLINES

Santa guides a PSA Boeing 727 into its assigned gate. Passengers flying Pacific Southwest Airlines never knew what to expect when they boarded a plane, and it was this quirkiness that made the airline such a popular carrier. (San Diego Air and Space Museum.)

ON THE COVER: PSA became famous for many things: inexpensive fares, friendly service, and its smiling aircraft. But to many, the airline would forever be associated with its beautiful flight attendants, known as "stews." In this photograph taken in the 1970s, PSA stews model uniforms from different eras in the company's history. They are in front of another legend, the DC-3. (San Diego Air and Space Museum.)

IMAGES
of Aviation

PACIFIC SOUTHWEST
AIRLINES

Alan Renga and Mark E. Mentges,
San Diego Air and Space Museum

ARCADIA
PUBLISHING

Published by Arcadia Publishing
Charleston, South Carolina

Printed in the United States of America

Library of Congress Control Number: 2010921994

For all general information, please contact Arcadia Publishing:
Telephone 843-853-2070
Fax 843-853-0044
E-mail sales@arcadiapublishing.com
For customer service and orders:
Toll-Free 1-888-313-2665

Visit us on the Internet at www.arcadiapublishing.com

*This book is dedicated to all those who lost their lives
in the crashes of PSA flights 182 and 1771.*

CONTENTS

ACKNOWLEDGMENTS

The authors would like to thank Katrina Pescador, Kathy Wright, Randy Prine, Stephanie Villar, Judy Bailey Garrett, Don Simoian, Gary Kissel, our editor Debbie Seracini, and all of the past employees of PSA! All images used in this book come from the archives of the San Diego Air and Space Museum.

INTRODUCTION

The story of PSA starts with Kenny Friedkin, a seasoned aviation instructor who operated a flight school at Lindbergh Field in San Diego after World War II called the Friedkin School of Aeronautics. After a few successful years of instructing veterans, the flight-school business began to slow down. Looking for other business opportunities, in 1949 Kenny made the fateful decision to start an airline. On May 6, 1949, a leased DC-3 taxied down the runway headed for Oakland, and a legend was born. Kenny named the carrier Pacific Southwest Airlines (PSA), but because so many navy men from San Diego flew on it, it soon would gain the nickname "Poor Sailor's Airlines."

From the start, PSA's business model was to offer low fares and quality service, exemplified in its first advertising slogan as "the World's Friendliest Airline." This model caught on, and soon PSA attracted more passengers than just sailors. The airline grew, both in terms of aircraft and destinations. Besides the flights from San Diego to Oakland, routes to Burbank and San Francisco were added. PSA was now in real competition with major carriers like United Airlines and Trans World Airlines (TWA), in some instances offering flights at half the cost. Additional DC-3s were followed by 70-passenger DC-4s in the mid-1950s. It was also during this decade that PSA started to earn the reputation for only hiring single, attractive stewardesses.

The next decade began with the introduction of an airplane that would become a PSA icon: the Lockheed Electra L-188. Although the 1960s was a decade of incredible growth, it began with a great loss as founder Kenny Friedkin passed away in 1962. Longtime PSA employee J. Floyd Andrews took over as president, a capacity in which he would serve until 1976. Another major event occurred in 1962, when PSA welcomed its one-millionth passenger on board. Growth and innovation were the themes of the first half of the 1960s, with PSA operating a new engine overhaul shop and a pilot training center; in addition, an automated phone-reservation system was put into service. Perhaps the biggest indication that PSA was coming of age was the addition of the 727 jet airliner in 1965. The latter half of the decade showed even more impressive expansion: new routes, new aircraft, and a new 185,000-square-foot administration and hangar complex. However, some might argue that the most important introduction PSA made in the 1960s was the unveiling of the first miniskirt stewardess uniform in 1966. The decade closed with the introduction of the famous smile on each PSA airplane, cementing in people's minds that PSA truly was the "World's Friendliest Airline."

If the 1960s was a decade of rapid growth, the 1970s was an era of success mixed with pitfalls. Spreading its wings, PSA ventured into the hotel and rental-car business. More routes were added and additional passengers were attracted to PSA, with each year setting new records. So confident were the PSA executives that they negotiated a contract for five Lockheed L-1011 wide-body jets. Unfortunately a rise in fuel costs, coupled with a slow economy, doomed the L-1011 venture, with only one seeing limited service with PSA. Yet the new president of PSA, Bill Shrimp (who was only the third to hold that position in the 25-year history of the airline up to that time), was able to weather the turbulent times, and soon both revenue and profit soared. With the Airline Deregulation Act of 1978, PSA finally was allowed to open routes to other states besides California. Soon PSA was servicing Nevada, Utah, and Arizona. For all of the ups and downs of the 1970s, the event involving PSA that would impact the minds of most Americans occurred on September 25, 1978. It was on this warm Monday morning when PSA Flight 182 collided with a Cessna 172 over San Diego, killing 144 people on the ground and in the air. Of those who died, 37 were PSA employees, which sent a shock wave through the airline's family. However, the airline quickly recovered, closing out the decade with record profits and passenger totals for 1979.

Perhaps a forbearer of what the 1980s would bring was the airline pilot strike of 1980, which lasted 52 days. Although settled in a relatively quick period, the strike perhaps indicated that the airline had outgrown its roots as a small organization where everyone worked together and made sacrifices. Yet revenue continued to grow for the first years of the 1980s, and with the introduction of new DC-9 Super 80 aircraft and the BAE 146-200, the number of total passengers served rose as well. Even more routes became available, including destinations in Oregon and Washington state. PSA even had flights to Mexico, making it an international carrier. However, 1983 proved to be a very bad year for PSA, as the airline lost money. It soon became apparent that the trend of airlines merging and increased competition might be too much for PSA to overcome. The era when an airline could offer low-cost fares and still provide friendly service had come and gone. As the decade drew to a close, the airline was sold to US Airways, and the last PSA flight took off on April 8, 1988.

However, the story of Pacific Southwest Airlines did not end there. The memories of those who worked for and flew on the smiling PSA jets live on. Each year, past employees still gather and recollect about the times they had at this unique company, which truly was a family. In addition, many individuals credit PSA as being the inspiration for successful airlines that operate today, such as Southwest, which offers discount fares and relatively friendly service. Hopefully *Pacific Southwest Airlines* will give the reader an insight into the airline and a time when flying was inexpensive, reliable, and enjoyable.

One

1940s

The Birth of an Airline

KENNETH FRIEDKIN

It is not an exaggeration to say that there would be no Pacific Southwest Airlines without Kenneth Giles Friedkin, known as Kenny, who was born in New York in 1915. As a child, Kenny was fascinated by the Barnstormers he watched perform, and they inspired him to become a pilot. He took his first flying lesson when he was only 17 and achieved his instructors rating at age 23. During the 1930s, he was the chief flight instructor and director of training at a flying school in Glendale, California. At the start of the World War II, Kenny trained a diverse group of pilots, including women who would ferry aircraft with the famed Woman's Auxiliary Service Pilots (WASPs) and Canadians who would fight the German Luftewaffe. In 1942, Kenny became a charter pilot for Consolidated Vultee's transport subsidiary, Consairway, before becoming a test pilot for Consolidated in San Diego. After the war, Kenny teamed up with friend Joe Plosser and opened the Plosser-Friedkin Flight School in 1946. A year later, Plosser sold his share of the school to Victor Lundy, and the school was renamed the Friedkin School of Aeronautics. It was this diverse background that would give Kenny the experience to become so successful in his future business ventures.

Kenny's wife, Jean, was an excellent partner—in marriage and in business. She had an integral role in Friedkin Aeronautics and later PSA, supporting the companies in many different capacities, from working in the office to serving as vice president. This relationship would be an indication that the PSA employees would be a family, in some cases literally.

Kenny Friedkin chats with two officers. Much of the Friedkin School of Aeronautics' clientele after World War II were former combat pilots who needed to obtain a civilian license in order to work in the growing airline industry. Many of these students paid for the lessons with their G.I. Bill benefits.

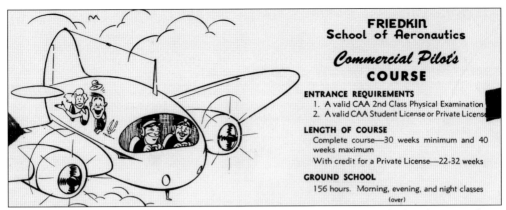

This advertisement for the Friedkin School of Aeronautics appeared in the local press and was handed out in the form of a business card. The school offered a variety of courses, including those for private pilots, commercial pilots, and flight instructors.

This Friedkin advertisement is for the private pilot course. The price for a private pilot course was $326, but the prospective student should not worry, because "convenient terms can be arranged."

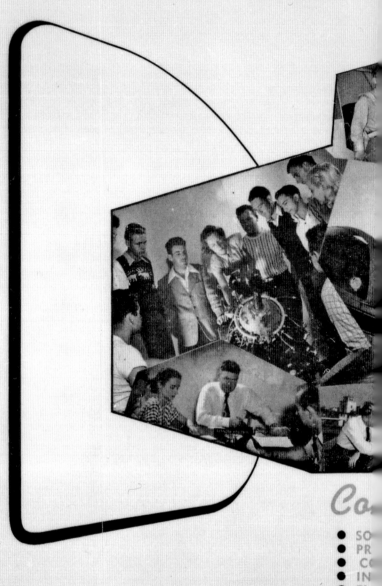

in
onautics

lete Courses

INING
PILOT'S LICENSE
CIAL PILOT'S LICENSE
ENT RATING COURSE
NSTRUCTOR'S RATING
GINE RATING

of this instruction upon request.

This brochure advertises the flight school at Friedkin Aeronautics and boasts that "flying is easier than driving a car." The prospective students would soon find out if this was the case. However, the claim that San Diego has some of the best flying conditions in the world is not an exaggeration. The area's ideal weather was what drew one of the pioneers of flight, Glenn Curtiss, to San Diego to establish his flight school in 1911.

This Fairchild PT-19 with an enclosed cabin was used at the Friedkin School of Aeronautics to train students. The school's aircraft would be put to good use, because at its height, more than 200 students were enrolled.

Here is a view of the Friedkin School of Aeronautics at Lindbergh Field taken from the rear. Note the original art deco passenger terminal to the right. Both buildings fronted Pacific Highway on the east end of the field, where Landmark Aviation now stands.

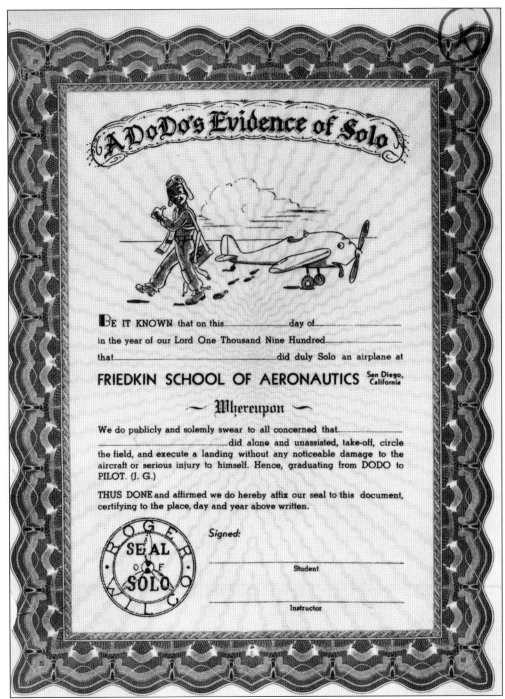

This certificate, called "A Dodo's Evidence of Solo," was given to students at the Friedkin School of Aeronautics on that special day when they made their first solo flight. This is an important day in a pilot's life, when a person symbolically gets off the ground and sheds his or her image of a flightless bird.

Before students could even set foot in an airplane, they had to spend many hours in a classroom. During ground school, the students would learn the basics of flight in addition to rudimentary aircraft mechanics. Notice the different items used for instruction, including engine parts and propellers.

A student sits attentively in Friedkin School's link trainer. The link trainer was known as the "pilot maker." Organ bellows and a motor provided movement to the trainer, which was mounted on a pedestal so the "airplane" could pitch, roll, dive, and climb as the student flew it.

From the beginning, PSA was not a male-only business; some of the first employees were women. Here Betty Lambert explains to students how a reciprocal engine functions at the Friedkin School. It is important to note that there are female students in this class as well.

The Friedkin School's Cessna Bobcat flies above San Diego Bay. Looking at all of the ships below, it is easy to see that there were many sailors in the area and that an airline to service their travel needs would be ideal. The two-engine Bobcat was used for pilot training but later was conscripted into service for charter flights when Friedkin decided to start an airline.

In this photograph taken in 1947, key members of Friedkin Aeronautics are seen in front of the company's hangar and aircraft. Kenny Friedkin is in the center; to the right of Kenny is Eleanor

"Fergie" Ferguson, the first official employee at Friedkin. She would go on to work for PSA until 1982 in a variety of capacities: link trainer instructor, bookkeeper, and eventually as treasurer of PSA.

During down time at the Friedkin School, students enjoy a game of ping-pong. Notice the parachutes in the background, which were a must for all aspiring pilots.

As the postwar demand for flying lessons by veterans began to trickle off, Friedkin used his aircraft in other ways to create revenue. One venture was a banner-towing business. Companies, such as American Cleaners, would be charged by the hour to have a large banner sporting their name flown above San Diego. Such banners are still a common sight around the area on summer days.

Another attempt at increasing revenue was by offering propeller service at Lindbergh Field. Unfortunately there were not enough blades that needed straightening to make the propeller division of Friedkin Aeronautics extremely profitable.

It soon became evident that, due to decreased demand, Friedkin Aeronautics could no longer survive as a flight school and banner-towing operation. However, it did have some success offering charter flights, so Kenny and instructor J. Floyd Andrews agreed to expand this service into an airline to offer flights from San Diego to the Bay Area. It was decided that the airline division of Friedkin Aeronautics would be called Pacific Southwest Airlines, and almost immediately the airline was called PSA for short. A 28-seat Douglas DC-3 was leased for $2,000 a month. On May 6, 1949, PSA made its first flight, offering service to Oakland, for a one-way fare of $15.60. And with that, a legend was born.

		FLIGHT RECORD FROM	TO MAY	1949	AND LOG								

DATE	AIRCRAFT FLOWN			FLIGHT		INSTRUMENT		NIGHT FLYING		SINGLE ENGINE		MULTI-ENGINE		DAILY
	MAKE AND MODEL	CERTIFICATE NUMBER	ENGINE	H.P.	FROM	TO	LINK TRAINER / RADIO or HOOD	DUAL (AS INSTRUCTOR / AS STUDENT) / SOLO	DUAL (AS INSTRUCTOR / AS STUDENT) / SOLO	AS INSTRUCTOR / AS 1st PILOT / STUDENT or CO-PILOT	TOTAL TIME			

Date	Make & Model	Cert. No.	Engine	H.P.	From	To	Instrument	Night Dual/Solo	Single Engine	Multi-Engine (Inst / 1st Pilot / Co-pilot)	Daily Total
APRIL '49	CESSNA T50	56609	JACOBS (2)	450	CALEXICO & IMET	(L)				1:30	1:30
" "	" "	"	"	"	S.A.N. – LOCAL					1:30	1:30
" "	AERONCA 7AC	1646E	CONT.	65	" "	" "			4:20		4:20
" "	"	1566E	"	"	"	"			4:45		4:45
" "	"	1920E	"	"	"	"			2:05		2:05
MAY 1	N.AMER. T-6	A.F.	WASP-PiW	650	"	"	(R) 1:30	2:15	5:45		5:45
5-4-49	DOUGLAS DC-3	60256	P & W (2)	2500	TORRENCE – S.A.N.					1:00	1:00
"	"	"	"	"	S.A.N. – LOCAL			:30	* 3 LANDINGS WITH LEONARD – :30		1:30
5-6-49	"	"	"	"	SAN-OAK-BUR-SAN			3:00		3:45 / 2:00	5:45
5-7-49	"	"	"	"	" "			3:35		3:00 / 3:00	6:20
5-8-49	"	"	"	"	" "		(W) :15	2:00		3:50 / 2:00	5:50
5-9-49	"	"	"	"	" "		(W) :15	2:45		2:00 / 3:50	5:50
5-13-49	" "	"	"	"	" " LAX		(W) 2:45	3:40		3:50 / 3:00	6:50
5-15-49	"	"	"	"	" BUR-OAK-BUR-SAN		(R) 1:15	5:00		1:00 / 3:30	6:30
5-18-49	"	"	"	"	LAMITA – S.A.N.		Hood – 1:00			1:30	1:30
5-26-49	"	"	"	"	SAN-BUR-OAK-BUR-SAN			1:00		3:40	3:40

I hereby certify that the foregoing entries are true and correct.

SIGNED Joseph B Plosser – ATR–57116
Pilot's Signature

							7:00	24:45	16:55	24:35 / 22:00	63:50
							222:50	397:10	2148:55	808:25 / 657:50	4588:50
							229:50 / 421:55		2165:50	830:00 / 679:50	4645:20

The pilot's logbook of Joseph "Bud" Plosser records the first PSA flight from San Diego to Oakland and back, with a stop off in Burbank. The total flight time was five hours and 45 minutes. Of interest is the entry "3 Landings with Leonard" that indicates "shake down flights" with copilot Leo Leonard. In addition, "P & W" is written in the engine column for the DC-3, which indicates the reliable Pratt and Whitney power plant was used.

San Diego had long been a navy town, and from the beginning Kenny Friedkin believed that sailors would be the perfect passengers for PSA. So many bell-bottoms flew on PSA that it soon gained the nickname "Poor Sailors Airline." At first, PSA only offered weekend flights between San Diego and Oakland, but soon daily flights and a stop off in Burbank were added.

PSA's first ticket booth started out with a less than glamorous function. It originally served as an outhouse for employees of Convair Aircraft at Lindbergh Field. However, with some paint and cleaning, the former porta-potty served as a more than adequate ticket counter.

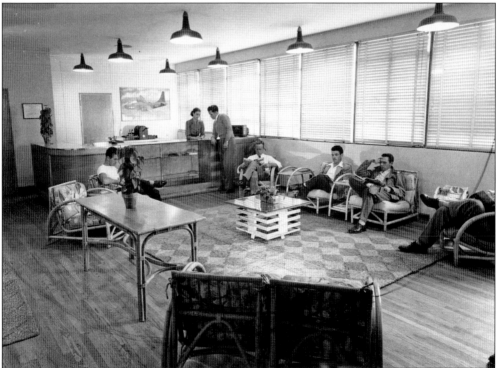

The early PSA waiting room at Lindbergh Field was about the size of a home living room, which was quite a contrast to the large, present-day terminal waiting areas. Pictured here is Eleanor "Fergie" Ferguson (PSA's first employee) behind the desk, talking with Gordon Tinker (seniority pilot no. 1).

From the start, PSA used the advertising slogan the "World's Friendliest Airline" and certainly lived up to this claim. It would be the flight attendants, known as "stews," who would be the face of the airline. Their job was to look after the safety and comfort of the passengers. They exuded the welcoming spirit, which would attract many celebrities to fly PSA throughout its existence. Here Hollywood starlet Mary Beth Hughes deplanes a DC-3 as Capt. J. Floyd Andrews and stewardess Ramona Currin look on.

From left to right, Bud Plosser, Ramona Tower, and Major Thom model the uniforms worn in the first days of PSA. A pilot, copilot, and solitary stewardess were the usual crew of the DC-3.

Two

1950s

GROWING UP

As the 1950s started, it became clear that the decade would be one of growth for PSA. Even though the cash position of the early airline was still "precarious" according to February 1950 board minutes (Kenneth Friedkin needed to borrow $2,000 from a friend to keep the airline running), finances would soon turn around. By 1951, the airline actually posted a profit of $6,093. Rising profits would be driven by the accumulation of additional aircraft, including the "Coffee-Can" DC-3, so called because it was in part purchased by contributions from PSA employees. By 1953, PSA had four DC-3s operating on a daily basis, which allowed it to carry over 115,000 passengers that year. PSA's reputation as an on-time airline providing friendly service was growing. And by offering fares at close to half the price of major carriers, it was attracting an increasing number of passengers. As the airline grew, additional routes were added, and larger aircraft joined the fleet. By the time the decade was out, PSA certainly showed little resemblance of the fledgling carrier that had been operating a single airplane.

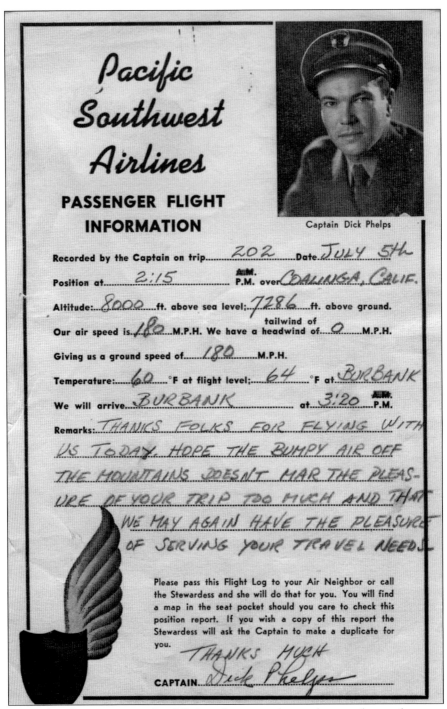

Pacific Southwest Airlines

PASSENGER FLIGHT

INFORMATION

Captain Dick Phelps

Recorded by the Captain on trip......_202_...... Date.._JULY 5th_..

Position at....._2:15_..... ~~A.M.~~ **P.M.** over _COALINGA, CALIF._

Altitude:.._8000_..ft. above sea level;.._7286_..ft. above ground.

Our air speed is.._180_..M.P.H. We have a ~~headwind~~ tailwind of.._0_..M.P.H.

Giving us a ground speed of....._180_.....M.P.H.

Temperature:....._60_..°F at flight level;.._64_..°F at _BURBANK_

We will arrive._BURBANK_....... at.._3:20_.. ~~A.M.~~ **P.M.**

Remarks:_THANKS FOLKS FOR FLYING WITH US TODAY. HOPE THE BUMPY AIR OFF THE MOUNTAINS DOESN'T MAR THE PLEASURE OF YOUR TRIP TOO MUCH AND THAT WE MAY AGAIN HAVE THE PLEASURE OF SERVING YOUR TRAVEL NEEDS_

Please pass this Flight Log to your Air Neighbor or call the Stewardess and she will do that for you. You will find a map in the seat pocket should you care to check this position report. If you wish a copy of this report the Stewardess will ask the Captain to make a duplicate for you.

THANKS MUCH

CAPTAIN._Dick Phelps_

Each captain handwrote a personalized flight information sheet to be passed around to passengers as some "entertainment" on early PSA flights. Occasionally ground speed on the flight was as low as 155 mph when flying up the California Central Valley during a three-hour, 35-minute flight from Oakland to San Diego—about twice as fast as present-day speedsters making the drive on I-5. This message is from Capt. Dick Phelps warning of possible turbulence.

PSA also utilized a hangar on the south side of Lindbergh Field for maintenance. Here a DC-3 (N17085) goes in the shop for some much needed work. Today the commuter terminal stands in this approximate location. For a while, Friedkin also worked on private airplanes like the Douglas C-46 in the foreground, but in 1952 this service stopped. Also in this year, the flight school was closed due to low enrollment in the courses.

PSA started service to San Francisco in July 1951, giving the airline a third destination. This ticket office, located in downtown San Diego, is offering a $15.44 fare to San Francisco. Larger carriers, such as TWA, United, and Western were charging $33 for the same flight.

The San Mateo Junior College football team poses in front of a PSA DC-3, which they chartered to fly from San Francisco to Orange County Airport. The Bulldogs played the Pirates of Orange Coast College in October 1952. According to press reports, the PSA flight was the best part of the trip for the Bulldogs, who lost to the Pirates 42-0.

On October 30, 1951, both engines of the DC-3 pilot Dick Phelps was flying suddenly quit just outside of Burbank. Phelps was forced to belly land in a field close to the air terminal. The 29 passengers and crew on board sustained only slight injuries. The plane was out of service for two months while being repaired, putting additional strain on the other two aircraft in PSA's fleet.

PSA mechanics pose at Lindbergh Field in the early 1950s. These mechanics were very busy, working sometimes around the clock to keep the old DC-3s in the air. Even though PSA had only three aircraft, their power plants were rotated so that they could undergo maintenance and overhaul.

A smiling stewardess boards a DC-3 while it is being refueled and restocked for flight. Passengers were treated to refreshments while in flight.

Skylines

PUBLISHED BY PACIFIC SOUTHWEST AIRLINES

| Volume 1 | OCTOBER, 1953 | Number 1 |

News Program Aired By Seymour Francis

Veteran newscaster Seymour Francis initiated his new PSA news program last month over radio station KSDO in San Diego. The terse, fifteen-minute newscast has found an immediate and receptive audience.

Francis, a long-time favorite with radio listeners in the area, has brought a balance of national, international and local news to his daily program.

LONG BEACH JOINS PSA SCHEDULE

LONG BEACH—This bustling oil and resort city welcomed the world's friendliest airline early this month with a celebration that seems destined to hold Western division honors for some time to come.

PSA added Long Beach to its route on October 1, and the next two days saw the Coast city extend greetings matched for warmth only by the 100 degree Santa Ana breeze that sent natives scurrying for the beaches. Civic officials, the Chamber of Commerce, business and industrial leaders and the press all cooperated to make the inaugural ceremonies a whopping success.

Mayor Clifford Rischell of Oakland led a parade of dignitaries from the Bay Area. Major newspapers, wire services and magazines in each city served by PSA sent representatives to join in the festivities.

Flown to Long Beach by PSA, the celebrants were greeted at the Wilton Hotel with a cocktail party arranged by Regal Pale Beer. They were PSA's guests at the hotel and for breakfast on Saturday morning.

After a tour of the city's industrial development, the visitors were hosted to a luncheon by the Long Beach Chamber of Commerce.

Toastmaster Howard Jones, assistant general manager of the CC, told the luncheon that the arrival of PSA was "one of the finest things that has happened to our city. We welcome this great airline and applaud its judgment to provide frequent, convenient service from Long Beach."

Mayor Rischell told the group that "Oakland is completely delighted with the wonderful service provided by this airline, and I'm certain that Long Beach will agree that PSA is truly the world's friendliest airline."

Vice Mayor Bazil Carleson of Long Beach extended the city's official welcome and said that he was "looking forward to many years of mutual growth from this new boon to our city. We are particularly gratified to have, for the first time, a direct air link with the Bay Area."

PSA now flies six daily flights into Long Beach. Initial reaction has been so heartening that Operations Manager J. F. Andrews said "plans are already being formulated toward the day when we will increase the number of flights to Long Beach."

Highlight of the inaugural ceremonies at the Wilton Hotel was a skit dealing with the evolution of the stewardesses uniform. Stewardesses Dana Price, Pat Sindelar, Sally Kordeleski, Billie Estergren and Nanette Grill modeled stewardess uniforms of the past, present and future.

Dana and Nanette wore uniforms as they might have been 50 years ago, at the birth of powered flight. Pat and Billie modeled uniforms as the might be 50 years hence, and Sally graced the current PSA stewardess uniform.

PSA Commuter Club Provides New Passenger Benefits

Publication of this first issue of PSA SKYLINES marks the birth of the PSA Commuter Club.

Open to all credit card holders, club membership entitles regular PSA passengers to monthly copies of **Skylines**, credit privileges and preferential reservation considerations when possible. Club members are also invited to offer suggestions for improving PSA service.

In welcoming club members President Kenny Friedkin said, "We're very happy to have you join the family of the world's friendliest airline, and we sincerely hope you will let us have your thoughts on how we can make your trips with PSA even more enjoyable and convenient."

The first issue of *Skylines* was written and edited by Kenny's wife, Jean, and was mailed to every PSA employee. *Skylines* gave the employees news about the airline and more personal stories about their fellow PSA family members. This first issue announces the addition of the Long Beach route, which was inaugurated with an elaborate ceremony. Unfortunately the Long Beach route was short lived and was discontinued in June 1954.

EFFECTIVE NOVEMBER 1, 1953

PACIFIC SOUTHWEST AIRLINE GUIDE

One of the SCHEDULED AIRLINES in the U.S.A.
(INTRA-STATE)

OAKLAND International Terminal LOckhaven 9-7017	SAN FRANCISCO 277 Post Street YUkon 2-4818 JUno 3-0931 PLaza 6-0660	LOS ANGELES Lockheed Terminal STanley 7-5437 CHarleston 8-1138	LONG BEACH Daugherty Field 40-8511 40-8613	SAN DIEGO Lindbergh Field Woodcrest 5-2105

DAILY — EXCEPT FRIDAY AND SUNDAY

Northbound	75	11	31	65
Lv. SAN	7:45	10:50	3:00	6:45
Ar. LB	8:25	11:30	3:40	7:25
Lv. LB	8:35	11:40	3:50	7:35
Ar. LA†	8:50	11:55	4:05	7:50
Lv. LA†	9:00	12:05	4:15	8:00
Ar. SF	11:00	2:05	6:35	10:00
Ar. OAK	11:20	2:25	6:15	10:20

Southbound	90	10	64	74
Lv. OAK	9:00	1:00	6:50	
Lv. SF	9:20	1:20	7:10	7:40
Ar. LA†	11:20	3:20	9:10	
Lv. LA†	11:30	3:30	9:20	
Ar. LB	11:45	3:45		9:50
Lv. LB	11:55	3:55		10:00
Ar. SAN	12:35	4:35	10:10	10:50

FRIDAY ONLY

Northbound	75	105	1	41	61	85
Lv. SAN	7:45	10:05	1:00	4:00	6:00	8:45
Ar. LB	8:25	10:45	1:40		6:40	
Lv. LB	8:35	10:55	1:50		6:50	
Ar. LA†	8:50	11:10		4:50		9:35
Lv. LA†	9:00	11:20		5:00		9:45
Ar. SF	11:00	1:20	4:20	7:00	9:00	11:45
Ar. OAK	11:20	1:40	4:00	7:20	9:20	12:05

Southbound	90	12	22	50	80	94
Lv. OAK	9:00	12:00	2:05		8:00	9:50
Lv. SF	9:20	12:20	2:25	5:00	8:20	10:10
Ar. LA†	11:20	2:20	4:25	7:00		12:10
Lv. LA†	11:30	2:30	4:35	7:10		12:20
Ar. LB	11:45	2:45	4:50		10:30	
Lv. LB	11:55	2:55	5:00		10:40	
Ar. SAN	12:35	3:35	5:40	8:00	11:20	1:10

SUNDAY ONLY

Northbound	105	1	41	61	85	15	131
Lv. SAN	10:05	1:00	4:00	6:00	8:45	10:50	1:30
Ar. LB	10:45	1:40		6:40		11:30	2:10
Lv. LB	10:55	1:50		6:50		11:40	2:20
Ar. LA†	11:10	2:05	4:50		9:35		2:35
Lv. LA†	11:20	2:15	5:00		9:45		2:45
Ar. SF	1:20	4:35	7:00	9:00	11:45	1:50	4:45
Ar. OAK	1:40	4:15		9:20	12:05		5:05

Southbound	12	22	50	72	94	122	210
Lv. OAK	12:00	2:05	5:20		9:50	12:30	2:30
Lv. SF	12:20	2:25	5:00	7:30	10:10	12:50	2:10
Ar. LA†	2:20	4:25	7:20		12:10		
Lv. LA†	2:30	4:35	7:30		12:20		
Ar. LB	2:45	4:50		9:40		3:00	
Lv. LB	2:55	5:00		9:50		3:10	
Ar. SAN	3:35	5:40	8:20	10:30	1:10	3:50	5:10

SAN DIEGO   LONG BEACH   LOS ANGELES   OAKLAND   SAN FRANCISCO

Light Face A.M. — Bold Face P.M.   Pacific Southwest Airlines   Local California Time
†Lockheed Air Terminal   Flies on Benrus Watch Time   Subject to Change Without Notice

PACIFIC SOUTHWEST AIRLINE FARES

San Diego—Oakland—San Francisco	$17.25		San Francisco—Oakland—Long Beach	$13.95
San Francisco—Oakland—Los Angeles	11.70		San Diego—Long Beach	4.80
Los Angeles—San Diego	5.55		Long Beach—Los Angeles	2.25

This early DC-3-era schedule chronicles the three-hour and 35-minute flight from San Diego to Oakland—the express service (without the Los Angeles stop) was "only" three hours. Note the San Diego to San Francisco fare of $17.25. According to the Department of Commerce official inflation calculator, that would be $132.32 in 2008 dollars each way. This author recently bought a $120 round-trip fare for the same route.

PSA garnered national attention in July 1953 when dispatcher William Golliher married stewardess Beverly Knowles on board a PSA DC-3. Kenny Friedkin and chief pilot Leo Leonard flew the airplane while vice president Mike Bogle played an organ, which was temporarily installed on the airplane. The wedding was a success, and the bride and groom enjoyed a long, happy marriage.

A PSA stewardess comforts the nervous bride. It is unclear if she is anxious about the impending ceremony or the turbulence, which the DC-3s were notoriously famous for.

Passengers are greeted with the typical PSA smile at the San Francisco ticket counter. Initially PSA had did not have an office space inside the terminal and operated from a temporary counter on the sidewalk. When Oakland was cut from the schedule in March 1954, San Francisco remained the airline's northern-most destination.

PSA opened a ticket office in downtown Los Angeles to reach more potential customers. A flight between San Diego and Los Angeles cost a little over $5.

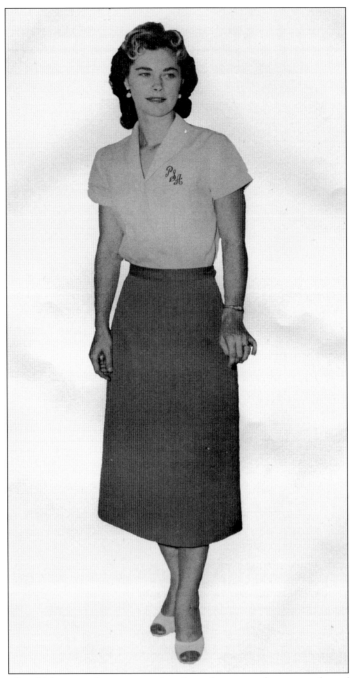

Not only were the flight attendants attractive, but also ground personnel, such as this 1950s station agent, were required to give "special attention to their appearance." The PSA station manual states, "Female personnel should give special attention to hands and hair; hair must be neatly combed, and pin curls or bandannas will not be worn." Agents were also required to buy their own uniforms. Uniforms required for women included a PSA green blouse (three minimum at $3.50 each), PSA regulation skirt (two minimum at $15 each), brown shoes, and PSA wings (furnished by the company).

Dana Price, seen here in the back of a DC-3, was named PSA's chief stewardess in 1952. As such, she was in charge of hiring and training the flight attendants.

Copilot Spencer Nelson, stewardess Betty Joe Cox-Elliot, and Capt. Doug Faulkner welcome passengers aboard their DC-3. It is interesting to note the star above the wings and the four strips on Faulkner's uniform, which denote him as the captain.

Capt. Leo Leonard and Carol Torgeson welcome a child afflicted with muscular dystrophy on board. From the start, PSA had a long history of offering flights at low or no cost to charitable organizations.

Five lovely PSA flight attendants model the green uniform, which was used in the early 1950s. PSA had strict guidelines for hiring flight attendants: they must be between the ages of 19 and 26, stand 5-foot, 3-inches to 5-foot, 7-inches tall, be a high school graduate, and be in excellent health with a good personality and neat appearance. Applicants could not be married, and if they wed, they could no longer work for PSA.

Elaine Jackson (right) and Maureen Ghio (left) pose with a Pan American stewardess in the mid-1950s. The PSA stews are wearing beige uniforms, which feature an elaborate monogram and fashionable hat. Before their first flight, stews attended ground school where they were trained in first-aid and map reading as well as given lessons in "poise and charm."

By 1955, it became clear that the DC-3s were too small and too slow to handle PSA's increasing passenger loads. In 1955, two DC-4s were purchased by PSA, and a third was purchased a year later. The four-engine DC-4 could carry twice as many passengers as the DC-3 and was over 70 mph faster.

Even though the DC-4s were new to PSA, they were already being retired by larger airlines such as United. In an effort to make the PSA DC-4's look newer, the windows were painted to resemble the square windows of the DC-6 aircraft. Note in this photograph the original round windows of this early PSA DC-4 and the square paint design. Although the DC-4s were slower than the newer (and more expensive) DC-6s, they were much faster than the old DC-3s, and in January 1956 PSA flight 702 set a new record for the San Francisco to Burbank route in one hour and 10 minutes.

SAFETY • COMFORT • DEPENDABILITY

4 Engine Service on ALL Flights and the Lowest Fares in the West

SAN FRANCISCO SAN DIEGO 15⁴⁴   SAN FRANCISCO LOS ANGELES 9⁹⁹   LOS ANGELES SAN DIEGO 5⁴⁵

all fares plus tax

Pacific Southwest Airlines A DIVISION OF FRIEDKIN AERONAUTICS

It would be very hard to argue that these fares were not the lowest on the West Coast. PSA marketed the fact that the DC-4 had four engines so that passengers would come to equate the additional engines with speed and safety.

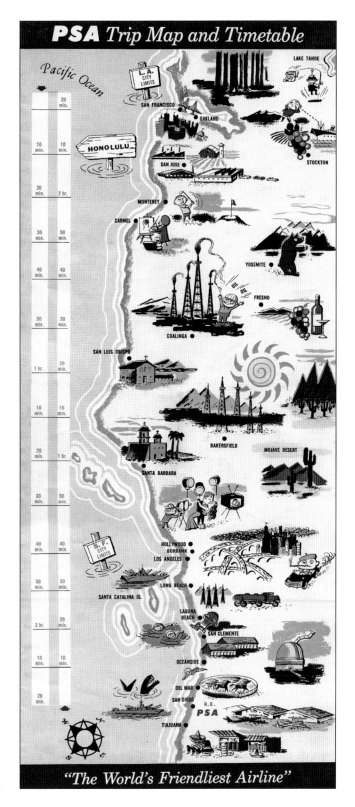

This brochure not only pointed out the highlights that California had to offer PSA passengers, it included a timetable so that travelers would know what landmarks they would be flying over at a particular time during a flight.

Throughout its history, PSA was known to be the favorite airline of celebrities of all shapes and sizes. Here Lassie deplanes from a DC-4.

Starting in 1956, San Diego celebrated the Fiesta del Pacifico, a monthlong celebration of Spanish and Mexican culture, which included plays, parades, and parties. PSA honored the fiesta by providing the stews with these special "south of the border" uniforms. The DC-4s were also decorated both inside and out while the fiesta was in progress.

In the days of the DC-4, waiting for the passengers brought out the entire PSA crew. A fourth DC-4 went into service with PSA in July 1957. The four aircraft were able to provide a schedule of 82 flights per week. In May 1958, the DC-4s would begin service at Los Angeles International Airport.

The growth of Lindbergh Field is evident in this photograph of the Friedkin Hangar taken in the late 1950s as the many cars in the newly paved parking lot show that the airport had become very busy. The DC-4 in the foreground has just completed routine maintenance. All four of PSA's DC-4s would be sold by 1961.

 *Skylines*

Pacific Southwest Airlines   April, 1957

MUSIC TO BE ADDED TO PSA FOUR-ENGINE FLEET

Music—the latest inovation for passenger luxury and comfort will be adopted by Pacific Southwest Airlines sometime within the next month, Kenney Friedkin announced.

The entire fleet of PSA's giant four engine airliners will be equipped with Travel Muzak* as an additional feature of the now luxurious service.

The new service will also be aimed at relieving fatigue, tension, and anxiety, a common problem of all public transportation organizations, according to a recent survey.

The heart of the flying music system is a tape reproducer no larger than a shoe box and weighing only 27 pounds. It was designed by the Presto Recording Corporation especially for service on planes, trains and other moving vehicles.

For the mechanically inclined, the new system can be described as follows: A unit consisting of a transport mechanism and a built-in preamplifier contained in a standard one-unit ATR enclosure which fits the standard air-

(Continued on Page 4)

And then there was music. . . . Stewardesses Dani Semon (left) and Elaine Block get set for the melodies which will float from PSA speakers in the near future.

Always an innovator, PSA offered music on some aircraft as early as 1957. Two hours of continuous background music was provided by a specially designed sound system from the Muzak Company, which overcame the piston-engine noise. This service was provided at no cost compared to today's airlines where in-flight entertainment is often an additional charge.

During the late 1950s, Kenny Friedkin looked at options to modernize PSA's fleet. He traveled to France to inspect the Sud-Aviation Caravelle, a twin-engine jet airliner. The company wanted to make a deal with PSA and flew a Caravelle into Lindbergh Field in 1957. This was the first commercial jet landing at the airport. Here two PSA stewardesses entertain two of their counterparts from Air France underneath the tail of the Caravelle.

After much consideration, Friedkin decided not to purchase the Caravelles. Instead, he opted for the Lockheed L-188 Electra, a 98-passenger turboprop airliner. PSA would eventually operate six of the Electras, which would be in service until 1968 (with a short renaissance in the 1970s). Here a Lockheed executive uses a model to show Kenny the fine points of the ship.

The Lockheed Electra added a third crew member in the cockpit, a flight engineer, who ensured that the engines were working properly. These men were enrolled in a PSA flight engineer training program sponsored by the airline in 1959 so that a full crew would be ready once the Electras were received.

The First Lockheed Electra, N171PS, was delivered to PSA on November 6, 1959. The Electras were much more comfortable than the DC-4s, as they were air-conditioned and pressurized. They also had two bathrooms and a kitchen area for food preparation.

The first flight of the Electra took place on November 20, 1959, and was flown by Kenny Friedkin himself. To prove that the Electra would greatly reduce flight times, he pushed the airplane to its limit and set a commercial airliner speed record of 24 minutes between San Diego and Los Angeles. Two more Electras were received by PSA before the end of the year.

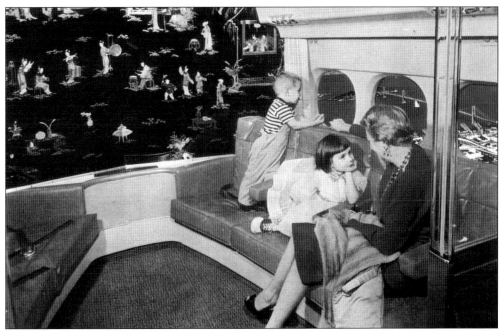

Jean Friedkin designed the interior of the Electras that featured cream, beige, and turquoise seats lined five across. In addition, there was a lounge in the rear of the aircraft consisting of five seats arranged in a semicircle. Here Jean and two of her grandchildren enjoy a flight over San Francisco.

Jean Friedkin also designed a new uniform to coincide with the introduction of the Electra. The new look consisted of a cocoa brown suit, a white blouse, and a small hat with flight wings on the side.

Three

1960s
COMING OF AGE

Like the decade that preceded it, the 1960s would be one of continued growth. Additional aircraft and routes would be added to PSA throughout the decade. Starting with a modest profit of $499 in 1960, every other year of the decade showed an increase in revenue. The high mark was in 1968 with the airline transporting almost four million passengers and generating revenue of over $57 million, of which $4 million was profit. In addition, the airline would branch out into other enterprises, including flight training and hotel operations. Perhaps the highlight of the decade would occur in 1968 with the dedication of a state-of-the-art headquarters and maintenance facility at Lindbergh Field. Exciting promotions would help PSA earn a national reputation as a fun, friendly airline. The 1960s would also include heartbreak, as the airline would lose its founder. However, by the end of the decade, it was quite clear that PSA had come of age and was a major player in jet-age air transport.

Two children peer out of the windows of a PSA Electra as the pilot just alerted them that Santa and his reindeer had been seen flying next to the plane during a Christmas flight. PSA put special effort into making sure that holiday travelers had a special experience.

A few minutes after the pilot announced the reindeer sighting, a PSA employee dressed as Santa would pop out of the cockpit and greet the younger passengers with candy canes and other sweets. Meanwhile, the older passengers would be treated to champagne by the stews.

Christmas was not the only holiday that was celebrated on PSA flights. On this Halloween flight, passengers received special trick-or-treat bags while being entertained by banjo player Dean Batchelor. Scenes like this demonstrate that flying on PSA was much more than a way to get from point A to point B; it was a thoroughly entertaining experience.

To handle the increased passenger load, a new high-tech reservation center was built by PSA at Lindbergh Field. The center handled calls from San Diego, San Francisco, Burbank, and Los Angeles on 27 phone lines. Not only did the reservationists take incoming calls, but they also would make outgoing calls to inform passengers if flight times had been changed.

In August 1960, a Douglas DC-6B was purchased and added to the fleet. That same year, service was offered to Oakland for which the DC-6 was used. The Oakland route was cancelled in March 1961, and the DC-6 was soon sold to Holiday Airlines.

This is a stock certificate that was issued to Kenny and Jean Friedkin in 1961. In September 1961, the PSA Board of Directors voted to increase the total shares of the airline's stock to 400,000. As the value of the stock increased throughout the decade, many of those who had been with the airline from the beginning finally saw a real profit, and their faith in PSA finally paid off.

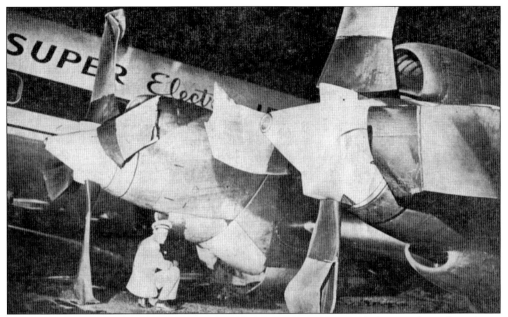

On December 27, 1961, an Electra in route from San Francisco with 93 people on board was diverted from Lindbergh Field to Gillespie Airport because of fog. Gillespie's taxiway could not handle the weight of the Electra, and the landing gear sank 3.5 feet through the asphalt, causing significant damage to the aircraft. PSA mechanics worked around the clock to get the Electra back in the air in just over 40 hours.

PSA stews pose in an advertisement for Pacific Telephone and Telegraph Company in 1962. The caption in *Skylines* to accompany the photograph read, "Where the pretty girls are! The Pacific Telephone and Telegraph Co. knows where to go for pretty girls when it completed the installation of the 'Golden Look' phone booths at Lindbergh Field: To PSA of course!"

Michael P. Bogle, a native of Spokane, Washington. Mike is the father of six children aged 6 to 14. When not flying, Mike sings lead roles in San Diego's Starlight Opera. Captain Bogle first began flying for the U. S. Navy, has been a PSA pilot since 1951.

Leland Corporon, an eight year Marine Corps veteran, joined the PSA flight staff in 1957. A native Californian from Long Beach, Captain Corporon is married and has one daughter. He is an enthusiastic golfer.

C. Donald J. Dolan has logged over 13,000 hours ing time and was a U.S. Air Force Instructor joining PSA in 1958. Don is intensely interes youth activities, and has the distinction of bei Manager of the 1961 Little League World Cham is married and has two children.

D. Douglas A. Faulkner has been flying for PSA 1951. He is one of the leading rifle marksmen United States, twice holding the title as Cal State Champion. Faulkner has also won the dent's Match, a top U. S. shoot. Doug is from G Colorado, is married and has three children.

E. Willis H. Holcomb, a PSA pilot since 1951, g flight training during his five years service wi Air Force in World War II. Captain Holcomb i Canton, Ohio, is married and has one child.

Spencer V. Nelson began piloting aircraft for PSA in 1951. Prior to that he was a flight instructor and served in the Navy in World War II. Spence is married, has three children, and spends his spare time ranching. He is a native of Illinois.

Milo L. Ott, a native of Payson, Utah, joined PSA in 1951 after flying as a co-pilot for TWA and Allegheny. Before his commercial experience, "Mike" Ott served five years in the Air Force. He is married and has three children.

B. D. Ray, another veteran of the Air Force, is originally from Oklahoma City. He has been a PSA pilot since 1957 and before joining PSA was a flight instructor. Captain Ray is married and has three children.

L. William R. Shimp, Assistant Chief Pilot, ha flying for PSA since 1949. In addition to his Ai port Rating, Bill holds a license as a commerci instructor. He served with the Air Force from 1946, is married, has three children, and is ec home in the cockpit or on the golf course.

M. Don Stevenson became a PSA pilot in 194 many years of military experience. In additio Air Transport Rating, Don is rated as a fl structor. He has two daughters.

N. Lee Thaxton, a native Californian, born in A Prior to joining PSA in 1958, Lee was a Apache Airlines, an Air Force pilot instructor, pilot and civilian pilot instructor, an aircraft in and is a licensed aircraft and engine mecha hobbies are model building, sailing, campi "do-it-yourself" projects.

F. **William A. Lake,** a former Naval Aviator and Lt. Commander in the Naval Reserve. Bill has been flying since 1941, joined PSA in 1957. Bill is married and hails originally from Chicago, Illinois.

G. **Leo L. Leonard,** PSA Director of Flight, joined PSA in 1947. Prior to PSA he was a pilot for Flying Tiger Airline. He is a U.S.A.F. Reserve pilot and flew B-29's and C-54's in the South Pacific during World War II. Captain Leonard is responsible for all PSA pilot training. He is married and has two children.

H. **Allan S. Lindemann** spent six years in the Navy and four and one-half years as a pilot instructor in the Air Force before joining PSA as a pilot in 1957. Allan is married and has two children.

O. **Gordon B. Tinker,** Chief Pilot, is a native of Long Beach, Washington. He joined PSA at its formation. Captain Tinker is fully rated as an airline captain and also assists in the continuous training of PSA flight crews. Captain Tinker is married and has three children.

P. **John R. Tucker,** a World War II veteran of both the Chinese and the American Air Force, became a PSA pilot in 1951. He is an ardent hobbyist . . . boats, planes, trains, and restoring aircraft. A pilot since 1937, Captain Tucker is married and has three children.

Q. **Robert H. Willbanks,** another Marine Corps veteran, became a PSA pilot in 1953 after serving as a flying school instructor and chief pilot. Bob is from Amarillo, Texas, is married and has two children.

This handout was given to PSA passengers when they flew on the Electras and gave a brief biography of each pilot in the airline. It is interesting to note that the majority of the PSA captains flew combat missions in World War II and Korea. But beyond that, it was a diverse group: Douglas Faulkner was one of the leading rifle marksmen in the United States, Donald Dolan was the manager of the 1961 Little League World Series champs, and Captain Bogle had six children and sang in the starlight opera.

On St. Patrick's Day 1962, Kenny Friedkin died unexpectedly from a cerebral hemorrhage at the young age of 47. It sent a shock throughout the entire PSA family, which would suffer another terrible loss when Jean Friedkin died a little more than a year later. Seen here are Kenny and Jean shortly before their deaths.

Upon Kenny's death, J. Floyd Andrews took over as president of PSA. Andrews had been a member of the famed Eagle Squadron during World War II as an American flying for Britain. He later joined the U.S. Air Corps, and after the war he joined Kenny's staff at Friedkin Aeronautics as a flight instructor and eventually served as chief of operations. He would remain president and chairman of the board until 1976.

In 1962, PSA partnered with SFO Helicopter Airlines to offer service to additional Bay Area destinations. A passenger could fly into San Francisco Airport on a PSA Electra and then transfer to a Sikorsky helicopter and be transported to downtown San Francisco, Oakland, Berkeley, or Sunnyvale.

J. Floyd Andrews and fellow PSA employees celebrate the delivery of another Lockheed Electra. The last of the six Electras on order was delivered in 1963.

Late in 1962, a new uniform was introduced, which soon gained the nickname of the "banana skin" because of its extra tight fit. The banana skin would prove to be one of the many risqué uniforms PSA stews would wear. Here Lynn Maracin (second from left) and Loretta Coppney pose with comedian Dick Van Dyke and Dan Blocker of *Bonanza* fame.

During a thick fog, which shut down the San Francisco Airport for nearly three days in December 1962, PSA was the only airline able to shift operations to nearby fog-free Half Moon Bay Airport, because its Lockheed Electra's were capable of landing on the short runway there. This incident gave PSA a great publicity boost, as it chartered busses from fog-closed San Francisco Airport to Half Moon Bay on a nearly nonstop basis. "As fast as one load of passengers was delivered, the bus filled immediately with incoming passengers and the seats never got cold." Post-fog reaction was filled with praise, as hundreds of thank you letters and phone calls were received by PSA.

In order for PSA's full schedule with quick turnaround times to be effective, maintenance on the Electras was done at night. Here PSA mechanics burn the midnight oil to ensure that the fleet is operating safely and efficiently in 1963, by which time the airline was operating six Electras. The PSA maintenance department earned such a good reputation that the U.S. Air Force contracted the airline to paint 11 T-38 jets.

PSA was a generous airline, which often undertook charitable causes. The airline sponsored free flights for underprivileged and handicapped children, and here boy scouts board a scenic flight around California. Not only were such flights the right thing to do, but they also provided excellent public relations opportunities.

President Andrews hands out scholarship checks to two worthy recipients. Throughout its existence, PSA encouraged young people to pursue education in math, science, engineering, and other aviation-related studies.

TRADER'S FOLLY

BAY MEADOWS, CALIFORNIA, DEC., 8, 1964, WILLIAM MAHORNEY UP
FRANNIE(2nd)   SIX FURLONGS   1:10:1   PO PO AGGIE(3rd)
YACHET FARMS, OWNERS   M. E. MILLERICK, TRAINER

"THE P S A PURSE"

Trader's Folly sprints to victory during the 1964 PSA Purse at Bay Meadow's Race Track. As PSA grew, so did its sponsorships and public relations opportunities.

In the summer of 1964, Andrews announced that PSA would purchase six new Boeing 727-100s, a jet airplane that seats 128 passengers. Oakland service was also restored for the third time that year.

The 727 utilized three jet engines, which enabled it to cruise at speeds above 600 mph. This greatly cut down flight time on the routes on which it was employed.

PSA charged passengers $13.50 for the San Diego-San Francisco flight on the 727, as this billboard advertises. This low price caused a fare war, forcing United and TWA to reduce their rates so that they could compete.

To coincide with the introduction of the 727, a new stewardess uniform was also unveiled. The new outfit included a light beige wool jacket and heart-shaped hat.

In 1966, PSA received permission from the Public Utilities Commission (the agency that regulated air traffic in California at the time) to serve the new San Jose Municipal Airport (now Mineta San Jose International Airport) for flights to Los Angeles. Pictured here are some of the first passengers lining up at the "new" 1965 terminal (now the location of terminal C) to board a Lockheed Electra for Los Angeles. Fares were $13.50 for prop and $19.85 for pure jet flights. Eventually flights to San Diego and Burbank were added. San Jose remained an important city for PSA until the airline was sold to U.S. Airways.

Miss California draws the name for a PSA contest from San Jose sales representative Jerry Shaw in an effort to draw attention to PSA's newest Bay Area destination.

Johnny Cash exits a PSA airliner in the late 1960s. The musician was one of the many famous personalities who flew PSA over the years that also included Bob Hope, Bing Crosby, and Milton Berle. Especially popular with the Hollywood crowd was PSA's Burbank flights, as the airport was located minutes away from Tinsel Town.

In mid-1965, PSA got back into the pilot-training business when it set up a program where the senior pilots taught younger pilots how to fly the 727. Soon this program became so successful that PSA started to train other airline's pilots. Pictured here are longtime PSA Captain Pappy Keough (in front, fifth from the right) and German Lufthansa Airline students. PSA started training 90 Lufthansa pilots in 1967 at a facility at Brown Airport in South San Diego. In addition, a flight-training class was set up at San Diego Mesa College, which was run by PSA instructors.

It was not all hard work for the students at PSA's Brown Field pilot-training facility. They could enjoy a swimming pool, gym, and tennis courts. In addition to the German pilots, PSA eventually trained students from All Nippon Airways and Japan Air Lines.

Starting in 1966, PSA periodically provided its employees with a Las Vegas getaway night. On the first trip, over 700 of PSA's 900 employees were flown to the resort destination, where they were treated to shows, dinner, drinks, and dancing. Many of the employees wore "Pure Sober Available" buttons with pure and sober crossed off!

In December 1966, PSA unveiled a new uniform that included an industry first: a miniskirt. The uniform was soft celery green with orange piping. A less obvious part of the new uniform was the orange ruffled petti-pants, which could only be seen from certain angles. PSA stewardesses were not allowed to be married in the early days, and if they did, they could lose their job. It was not until well into the 1970s that PSA followed the lead of other airlines and finally relented and allowed their stewardesses to marry. Of course, many stewardesses married secretly. This was the case for the married Miss PSA, Judy Bailey Garrett (right), when she applied for a passport under her maiden name in order to visit troops in Vietnam. She finally got "the secret and confidential help" of a PSA government relations officer to expedite her passport.

PSA stews show off their new petti-pants in front of the California State Capitol in 1967. The airline began service to Sacramento in February 1967. This was a very popular destination for California lawmakers, who often were called to the capitol building on short notice.

PSA president J. Floyd Andrews inspects a DC-9 with Douglas factory executives. PSA accepted its first DC-9 in 1967 but utilized the aircraft several times throughout its remaining existence.

The new jets PSA utilized required a crew of four flight attendants. For the first time, PSA hired men (who were called stewards) to fill out the four-person quota. Here PSA president J. Floyd Andrews poses with the first stewards to complete training.

During the Vietnam War, many soldiers used PSA for their travel needs. PSA not only supported the soldiers by giving them flights but with helping their morale as well. Here the airline welcomes Bob Hope's USO (United Service Organization) tour to San Diego as Raquel Welch (left) enjoys a laugh.

During the Vietnam War, members of the 174th Assault Helicopter Company wrote to PSA asking for pictures of Miss PSA, Judy Bailey. Judy's picture had been on billboards, the PSA flight magazine, ticket holders, and even trucks to advertise the airline. When it was discovered that she had been made the mascot for squadron VR 7 in Saigon, she was invited to visit the troops as a special guest of the surgeon general's team, flying around on a large Huey helicopter in mid-1967.

During Judy Bailey's Vietnam trip as Miss PSA, she visited field hospitals to comfort the wounded, spent time at the USO, and attended some formal dinner parties hosted by a general's group. When she started her visit, she was put in green army fatigues, but after the first day "the guys requested I ditch the fatigues and wear my miniskirt, which I did, complete with 3-inch heels."

Among the celebrities that flew PSA was then governor Ronald Reagan, posing here with three PSA flight attendants. Reagan was such a frequent PSA passenger that he received an honorary flight certificate from the airline in 1968 for having flown over 50,000 miles.

In 1968, the first PSA Boeing 737 went into service. The airplane could seat 112 passengers in comfort and received the nickname "Fat Albert" because of its short, stout appearance. Eventually PSA would operate 11 of the 737s. The introduction of the new Boeings allowed PSA to add Ontario as a destination in 1968 and to sell its remaining Lockheed Electras, making it an all-jet airline.

A PSA Jets team member scrambles for the ball. All of the players on the Jets were PSA flight attendants. Formed in 1968, the team would play exhibition games before or during halftime at NBA games. Opponents included disc jockeys, newspaper reporters, and the San Diego Chargers. In order to ensure victory, a memo urged the players to, "Practice, shape up, and diet!"

Members of the Jets pose in this team portrait. It is quite evident that these uniforms were the most revealing of any worn by PSA employees.

President Andrews gave longtime employee Ray Jacket a check to hand to Boeing executives in Seattle in return for a new 737. From then on, the 737 was known as "Ray Jacket's airplane."

This is a cutaway drawing of PSA's 185,000-square-foot combination hangar and three-story administration building, which was completed in June 1968. As the airline's fleet and operation grew, it became evident that larger facilities were needed. The building was located on the west side of Lindbergh Field's runway and could house three 727s. The building is currently used as the commuter terminal by American Eagle and United Express.

At the official ground-breaking for the new PSA administration and maintenance facility, beauties surround president J. Floyd Andrews. Such were the perks of life at the top at PSA.

A reconstruction of the original PSA ticket booth (the onetime latrine) is moved into position at Lindbergh Field. The ticket booth was used to show employees at the new hangar dedication how far PSA had come in such a short time.

Three PSA jets undergo routine maintenance inside PSA's new hangar. The large, well-lit facility allowed PSA mechanics to work around the clock to "keep em flying!" In addition to office and hangar space, the facility housed a jet-simulator training room, where students could learn to fly the 737 and 727 before actually taking to the air.

This is the PSA hangar facility is as it appears from the air. The view shows what an impressive structure it is. The old PSA hangar dating from the 1940s can be seen to the right.

PSA purchased the Valcar Rental Car Company in 1968, so it was certainly a busy year for the airline. PSA passengers were encouraged to rent from Valcar, and in many cases were given discounts if they did so. Here miniature ponies pull a small wagon to bring attention to the new merger.

To alleviate overcrowding due to increased passenger demand at LAX, in December 1969 PSA began to offer flights to Long Beach Airport. These lucky young men get to enjoy a piece of the extra large cake that was served to commemorate the event.

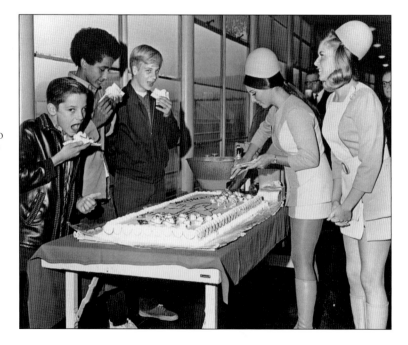

This cartoon, which appeared in a 1982 edition of *Skylines*, depicts the more aggressive nature PSA needed to maintain during the "dog eat dog" era of deregulation. The famous smile on each PSA aircraft dated from 1969, when one was painted on a plane for a television commercial. So fixed was "the smile" in the minds of Californians that when the *Los Angeles Times* published a cartoon of the space shuttle Columbia landing in California, complete with a "the smile," no one needed to explain.

"Just paint a smile, Jenkins!"

C. E. "Pappy" Keough (center) and copilot Leonard Dolan (second from right) stand in front of the helicopter they used to attempt to break an endurance record in 1969. The attempt was sponsored by local radio station KFMB. Not only did Pappy break the record, he bested it by 20 hours, staying aloft for 121 hours. Here they pose with the dedicated team of PSA technicians who kept their chopper fueled and lubed, as well as provided the flight crew with food as they hovered a few feet off the ground. The helicopter was a Bell 47G4, which was standard except for the inclusion of a specially constructed folding board that the pilots could use to get some much-needed rest.

PSA entered a dune buggy in the 1969 Baja 1000 Road Race, which ran from Ensenada to La Paz in Baja California, Mexico. The race was run on an 832-mile course, the majority of which was off-road. The PSA entry was refueled by helicopter to save time. Even though they did not win, the entry inspired other PSA employees to create a group dedicated to off-road adventuring.

The crew of the PSA entry into the Baja 1000 Road Race is posing by its car. Airline employees working on a volunteer basis built this car entirely in the PSA engine shop.

One of the most unique sagas in PSA history was the infamous Midnight Flyer, which began in 1969. The postal service asked PSA to connect Northern and Southern California with a late-night flight to carry mail and would subsidize the service. Because of the subsidy, PSA could charge a low $9.70 fare between San Francisco and Los Angeles. PSA did not think such a late flight would be popular and thus did not take reservations. Much to their surprise, sometimes several hundred people would show up for only 158 seats. The service was suspended for a few years in late 1978 when the flight was hijacked but put back into service in 1982.

Three PSA flight attendants are presented $100 bills by PSA president J. Floyd Andrews for winning the "Flight of the Month" award. Mystery passengers boarded many PSA flights and filled out ballots rating the stewardesses. One of the items the passengers rated was their "appearance." It is highly unlikely that this sort of competition would be allowed to go on today.

The old PSA hangar, which serviced the airline's first aircraft, was torn down at the end of the decade, which might be seen as symbolic of the changes the airline would undergo in the 1970s.

Four

1970s
AN INDUSTRY ICON

While the 1970s was a decade of uncertainty for many in the United States, it was one of stability for PSA. Passenger totals steadily increased, as did revenue. New routes were added, including the first interstate flights offered by the airline. New subsidiaries were also added; some obviously related to flight, others not as much. Certainly PSA's status as a cultural icon was solidified, and its reputation for inexpensive fares, friendly service, and beautiful flight attendants spread throughout the United States. Ambitions were high—perhaps a bit too much—as shown by the acquisition of L-1011 wide-body jets, which would lose the airline money. Unfortunately the decade would also contain the most tragic and heartbreaking day in the history of PSA, the crash of flight 182. Through all of the ups and downs, one thing is certain about the 1970s: if anyone saw a smiling airplane, they knew it belonged to PSA. The airline had become an American icon, as did their stews, shown here modeling various PSA uniforms.

A new decade brought on a new uniform. In 1970, PSA unveiled its most revealing stew uniform yet—a very short miniskirt worn over even shorter shorts. The uniforms were apricot and pink and could be accessorized with two different types of hats, along with matching luggage and shoes.

Shamu at Sea World San Diego shows his approval of the new uniform. Shamu was the stage name for the various orcas that performed at the marine-themed park, which opened in 1964. Sea World was one of the most popular destinations in San Diego, and as such, PSA often partnered with them for special promotions.

The 390-foot tall SkyTower, which was built at Sea World San Diego in 1969, was an instant advertising opportunity for PSA. Pictured here in the early 1970s is a group of "stewardesses" in front of the revolving passenger capsule. The tower with its huge PSA logo could be seen for miles on a clear day, and many locals referred to it as the "PSA Tower."

The pilot-training program was so successful that it had outgrown the Brown Field facilities. In 1970, PSA opened a second facility at Litchfield Airport in Phoenix, Arizona, for Lufthansa trainees. The Japanese pilots would continue to be trained at Brown Field until 1974. Luckily for the Lufthansa pilots, the PSA facility included a pool to cool off in during the hot days in the desert.

PSA was an early convert to "clean engines" and the reduction of noise pollution. Pictured here is a before and after shot in 1970 of a jet with "burner cans" fitted onto its Pratt and Whitney engines. These devices allowed better combustion and were installed on all of the aircraft, thus becoming the first "non-smoking" airline. Also, PSA worked with the city of El Segundo (near LAX) and San Diego to reduce noise pollution by reducing power requirements for takeoffs. El Segundo recognized PSA's efforts in a public thank-you letter.

PSA received competition from another intrastate airline in 1967, Air California. At first, Air California flew only between the Orange County Airport and San Francisco, because PSA did not fly that route. However, in 1970, Air Cal added San Diego as a destination and became a fierce competitor of PSA. Air Cal attempted to copy PSA's business model, and they even attempted to hire attractive stewardess of their own, as this photograph shows. The reader can judge if they were successful in this endeavor.

In 1970, executives at a newly created airline in Texas asked PSA president Andrews to help them in establishing their airline. Andrews befriended the executives and allowed them to send employees out to see how PSA did things. The Texans took copious notes and decided to implement much of what they saw working at PSA in their operations. Which airline was that? Southwest, which today carries more passengers than any other airline in the world and promotes itself as a low cost, friendly airline—sound familiar?

During most of the Vietnam War, PSA would launch "Operation Mistletoe" during the holidays. Operation Mistletoe was a series of parties for wounded veterans at military hospitals in San Diego, San Francisco, and Oakland. The vets would be treated to food, beer, champagne, and, perhaps most importantly, dancing with the stews.

In 1970, PSA flew 12 SLOBB (Stop Littering Our Beaches and Bays) members to San Francisco to demonstrate beach-cleaning techniques. Not only was this a good PR opportunity, it showed the airline's early interest in being green.

Unlike its larger interstate competitors United and Western Airlines, PSA was an intrastate carrier operating only in California, until 1978. The California Public Utilities Commission, the same commission that regulates electric utilities, regulated PSA. This billboard campaign around 1970 was to pressure the commission for additional service and cities. Because the California PUC set fares (not the federal government), PSA could charge less than its larger competitors, thus giving them a home-state advantage.

In 1970, construction commenced on the Islandia Hotel in Mission Bay. This was the first part of PSA's ambitious venture into running hotels, which would complete the "sleep" portion of their "Fly-Drive-Sleep" program. PSA bought Islandia Hotel and remodeled the existing 105 rooms and built a 266-room high-rise tower.

The Islandia Hotel was quite the resort with its restaurants, banquet facilities, and a conference center. It catered to fisherman and had a 250-slip marina as well as three sportfishing boats. Here J. Floyd Andrews, an ardent fisherman, christens the *Scat 1*, one of the Islandia's catamarans.

The "Fly-Drive-Sleep" program was not limited to San Diego. PSA also acquired, and then remodeled, the historic San Franciscan Hotel on Market Street. The hotel was originally built after the great 1906 earthquake and was a San Francisco landmark. After an extensive face-lift, its 430 new rooms were reopened in 1973 under PSA management.

Perhaps the most unusual part of PSA's "Fly-Drive-Sleep" program was when the airline leased the 400-room hotel portion of the *Queen Mary* from the City of Long Beach. In addition to stately rooms, the *Queen* featured restaurants, a museum, and Jacques Cousteau's Living Sea exhibit. PSA opened the hotel to visitors in 1973 with a gala party and operated it until 1980.

The airline's fourth hotel was the 365-room PSA Hotel Hollywood Park. The hotel was across the street from the Hollywood Park racetrack and the Forum, the home of the Lakers. The hotel was only eight minutes from Los Angeles International Airport and was a perfect location for the "Fly-Drive-Sleep" program. Construction of the hotel was completed in 1973.

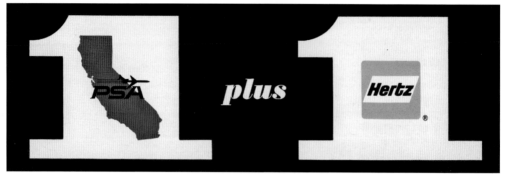

In 1971, Hertz rental car took over the drive portion of the "Fly-Drive-Sleep" PSA program from Valcar. With Hertz, PSA passengers could obtain a rental car while still in flight.

The most far afield subsidiary that the airline created was PSA Broadcasting, Inc., which acquired four radio stations in California—KPSA in Los Angeles, KPSE in San Diego, KPSJ in San Jose, and KPSC in Sacramento. Here PSA Broadcasting general manager George Whitney explains the automated music system to receptionist Denise Brown at KPSA, which played "music, only for a woman . . . the type of music a woman will find pleasing, both for work and for pleasure." It was hoped that the radio stations would not only be profitable but would serve as an advertising tool for PSA.

Members of the third-floor administration department are all smiles. This is with good reason, for in 1971 PSA offered many of its employees a 40-hour, four-day workweek—the first airline to do so. Since then, many other companies have copied this model.

Smokey the Bear is greeted by Islandia Hotel desk clerk San Hausman (left) and PSA stewardess Kathy Cady at the Western States Conference of Forestry at the hotel. PSA strove to hire attractive women to work for all of its subsidiaries in addition to employing the best-looking stewardesses.

In January 1972, the PSA "Midnight Flyer" to Los Angeles was hijacked to Cuba by a man and woman who smuggled guns aboard in their baby's cradle. The crew, held hostage at gunpoint (passengers had been let go), flew on to Havana, where the hijackers were eventually taken into custody. A second PSA hijacking later that year resulted in the death of a passenger and two hijackers and prompted the FAA to upgrade airport detection devices around the country.

RELAYING HIJACKERS ORDERS—The pilot of a Pacific Southwest Airlines Boeing 727 gave instructions he received from two armed hijackers to a maintenance man during refueling of the plane in Tampa, Fla., before continuing to Havana, Cuba.

(AP wirephoto)

Cross-country hijack ends safely in Havana

MIAMI (AP) — Seven stew-   Dianne was still rubbing her   pared to return to California.

PSA once again brought Northern and Southern California a little closer by symbolically transporting the first load of bricks for the repaving of San Francisco's Market Street. Here two PSA stewardesses are joined by Higgins Brick Company executives from Torrance, California, for the occasion in 1971.

In July 1972, two more destinations were added to PSA's already busy schedule: Fresno and Stockton. In addition, PSA replaced the red and white paint scheme on its airplanes with fuchsia, orange, and red stripes. To match their planes, a new hot pink uniform was introduced.

In November 1973, the first labor strike against PSA took place, when over 400 mechanics were joined by operations personnel in a monthlong walkout. Up until this time, PSA was known as a "family airline," and labor strikes were unthinkable. PSA managed to maintain most of its schedule, because other employees volunteered to do jobs left vacant by the strike. Pictured here is the severe damage done to one of the two Boeing 727's parked overnight at Los Angeles. The interior of one plane had been set on fire, and the other plane had seats slashed and liquid poured onto controls. Although the FBI investigated, no one was ever arrested, and it was not known if the damage was related to the strike. The strike ended before Christmas, but bad feelings between employees and management continued for years afterwards.

Pictured here in 1974 (the airline's 25th anniversary), PSA's 50 millionth passenger is honored as part of a tradition. Starting in 1962, the one millionth passenger was honored. Usually the passenger would receive two round-trip tickets and a sort of "gag gift," which could be anything from an extra large salami to a 6-foot-tall Snoopy. Here the lucky winner receives champagne, a 5-foot-long loaf of French bread, and a "date" with the flight attendants.

This picture of Bob Crane (of television's *Hogan's Hero's* fame) appears in the 25th anniversary edition of *PSA Magazine* with the caption, "It's easy to have fun aboard PSA flights." It may be difficult for airline passengers today to understand the affection Californians had for PSA, but low fares, friendly service, beautiful women, and the fun spirit of carefree California made PSA a local favorite. Ten years after the demise of PSA, the "famous" orange luggage tags that PSA gave to their business customers were still a familiar site at California airports. Even today, former PSA customers display a few of these tags with a sense of loyalty and pride.

In 1974, PSA received two 302-seat Lockheed L-1011 Tristars. It was hoped that the airline could turn around the jumbo jet as quickly as their smaller airplanes, which would lead to increased revenue. However, the jumbo jets came at the wrong time. Increased fuel costs and a recession meant a decrease in air travel. As a result, after only a few months of service, the Tristars were grounded until they were leased in 1978. PSA cancelled their order for three other Tristars with Lockheed. The L-1011 venture cost PSA millions.

Because PSA's L-1011 flights did not serve food due to their brevity, the airplane's galley was converted to a lower lounge where passengers could enjoy a drink and the famous PSA customer service.

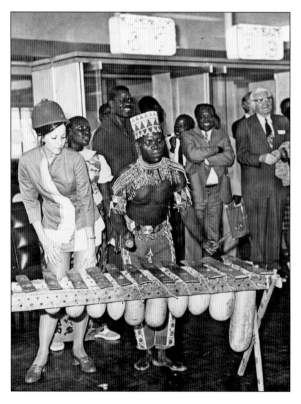

Before the second L-1011 went into service, it was flown around the world on a 32-day trip. After spending nearly a week at the Farnborough Air Show, the jet visited 24 cities in 21 nations. Twelve PSA stewardesses accompanied 100 Lockheed employees on the trip.

Since its inception, PSA had a reputation of hiring the best mechanics, and as such, many other airlines contracted their engine overhauls with them. The business was so lucrative that a subsidiary was created called Pacific Southwest Airmotive. In 1974, a new state-of-the-art building for the Airmotive branch was erected in the Mira Mesa area of San Diego. Engines for 727s, 737s, and even the L-1011 were overhauled at this facility, and customers included Mexican, Hughes Air West, and Braniff. During the 1970s, PSA employed over 400 mechanics in all areas, from the sheet metal shop to jet engine repair. Mechanics were always on duty 24 hours a day, but to maximize flying time, most repairs and upgrades were done in the middle of the night.

In 1975, it was "back to the future" for PSA when air service to Lake Tahoe was started. Due to local noise restrictions at the Lake Tahoe Airport, pure jets were banned from use, so PSA brought back four "ancient" Lockheed L-188 Electras. These were the airplanes that made PSA popular in its early days, and many passengers and flight crews had good memories of the propeller-driven aircraft. The planes were so popular with crews that fun names were given to each plane, such as Prince, Annie, and Cindy. The service to Tahoe was short lived, as high maintenance costs for the aging Electras and competition from other airlines forced PSA to end service in 1979. The Electras were retired that same year.

In March 1976, J. Floyd Andrews resigned as CEO of PSA after a tenure of almost 15 years. Bill Shrimp, who had risen up the PSA ranks since becoming an instructor at the Plosser-Friedkin school after World War II, replaced him. That year would also be the last in which PSA would utilize the 737.

Since the mid-1970s, PSA had offered the "mini-stews" program to San Diego teenage girls. The mini-stews learned the intricacies of being a flight attendant or operation agent. They received CPR training and were interviewed as if they were applying for a real job. Many of the mini-stews eventually found employment with PSA. In addition, an Air Explorer Scout Post was formed to introduce young perspective pilots to ground school.

By 1976, stewardesses had given way to flight attendants, and men had also joined the ranks. Gone were the popular orange and pink miniskirts and in came these "look of today" uniforms. Although many PSA employees liked the more professional look, many male customers grumbled about the loss of the miniskirt, and one San Francisco reporter said the flight attendants looked like "a gaggle of saving and loan vice presidents."

PSA was at the forefront of computerization, integrating its entire operations, including reservations, accounting, and maintenance. By 1976, PSA had over 40 individuals working in its computer services department. This is a vintage picture of "The Brain," as it was labeled, with Henry Diamond operating the new IBM 370/148.

In late 1978, PSA unveiled a new technological advancement called an automatic ticket machine. With the use of a credit card, a passenger could pay for a ticket to numerous PSA destinations. Today such machines are commonplace.

PSA MONTEREY SERVICE GRANTED BY PUC

Monterey will soon become PSA's thirteenth destination as the California Public Utilities Commission (PUC) granted the airline authority to serve the Monterey Peninsula Airport, during a recent meeting in San Diego.

The PUC authorized PSA to provide nonstop service between Monterey, San Francisco and Los Angeles, with through and connecting service to other PSA destinations.

Noted for its spectacular scenery, historical sites and golf courses, the Monterey Peninsula has been a major California vacation spot for many years.

According to Bill Shimp, president and chief executive officer, PSA officials are currently negotiating for space at the Monterey Peninsula airport, so no inaugural service date has been set at this time.

Monterey will become the first new city added to the PSA route system since South Lake Tahoe service began in April, 1975.

MONTEREY BEAUTY - Spectacular scenery such as the famed Fisherman's Wharf has made Monterey one of the premier California vacation spots. In addition to the scenic beauty, Monterey features many California historical sites and some of the state's outstanding golf courses.

In June 1978, PSA added Monterey as a destination, and passengers were free to enjoy the beauty of Canary Row and Carmel. However, the route would be short lived, and service would be cancelled in May 1979 to release aircraft for more popular routes.

The saddest day in the history of PSA occurred on September 25, 1978. PSA Flight 182 collided with a privately owned Cessna 172 over San Diego. All 135 on board the 727 were killed, along with the two men in the Cessna. In addition, seven people on the ground were killed, and 22 homes were destroyed or damaged. This disaster is still the worst aircraft accident California has seen.

IN LOVING MEMORY
AND TRIBUTE TO
THOSE 37 PSA EMPLOYEES
WHO LOST THEIR LIVES
WHILE SERVING OUR AIRLINE
SEPTEMBER 25, 1978

BILLY ADAMS
ROBERT BENNER
BARBARA BOISSELLE
KAREN BORZEWSKI
ARNOLD CALIFF
LYNN CHERRY
MARTHA COLEMAN
RICHARD CONWAY
LISA DAVIS
TIMOTHY DeLUCCA
JERI DICKSON
JAMES DORMER
JAVIER ESCALANTE
AMANCIO ELIZAGA
MICHAEL FITZGERALD
KATE FONS
GAIL FORSYTH
ROBERT FOX
STEVE HENRY

JIMMIE KELLY
COLLEEN KEPLER
BRIAN MACLEAN
DEBBI McCARTHY
JAMES McFERON
WHILHELMINA MOTTOLA
SPENCER V. NELSON
LYNN OWENS
BOB RAMIREZ
MARLA SCAVIA
GALE SHAPIRO
DON ST. GERMAIN
HERB STEWART
MARTIN WAHNE
ROGER WALSH
WILLIAM WHITE
JANE WHYLE-SPITZ
DEE YOUNG

Compounding the tragedy of Flight 182 was the fact that 37 PSA employees were on the airplane. In addition to the 727's regular crew, many employees had been commuting on the flight from Sacramento via Los Angeles. No PSA employee was unaffected by the accident. However, the PSA family regrouped after the devastation and grew closer than ever. Those lost are still commemorated each year by past employees.

The aftermath of the Flight 182 disaster did have a positive outcome. The events leading up to the accident were closely studied, and as a result numerous changes were made to how the airspace around airports is controlled, making the skies safer.

On October 24, 1978, the Airline Deregulation Act was signed into law. One result of this law was that PSA was free to offer flights outside of California. The first intrastate destinations were in Nevada.
In December 1978, PSA offered flights to Las Vegas and Reno.
A few months later, service was inaugurated to Phoenix, Arizona.

This cartoon, which appeared in *PSA Skylines*, takes a humorous look at a serious topic. Executives had long suspected that Amtrak (which is federally funded) was charging passengers much less than their operating costs. For example, Amtrak charged $8 for a San Diego to Los Angeles fare, but the real cost was estimated to be closer to $20. This undercutting boasted Amtrak's numbers, justifying its existence. Protests to government regulatory agencies from PSA fell on deaf ears, and many passengers took the cheaper subsidized train rather than flying.

THERE'S GOING TO BE A LOT OF SMILES AROUND SALT LAKE CITY.

PSA ANNOUNCES NONSTOP SERVICE TO LOS ANGELES FOR $70.

On November 7, 1979, service to Salt Lake City, a fourth out-of-state destination, commenced. During the first month of service to Utah, PSA carried close to 10,000 passengers to the state. Many of the travelers went there to enjoy skiing at the resorts around Salt Lake City.

Two major aspects of San Diego's aviation history are captured in this photograph. When a fire destroyed the San Diego Aerospace Museum in 1978, the community rallied to rebuild it better than ever. One of the first efforts in this rebirth was to replace the *Spirit of St. Louis* replica, which was destroyed. Here that replica flies past a PSA 727 on its inaugural flight in 1979.

SMILE HOUR

BEVERAGE SERVICE

Have we got smiles for you!
PSA invites you to sit back and smile it up all the way there
with a refreshing drink or two.

$1 COCKTAILS $1

If you would like two drinks, please order both at the same time.

scotch	brandy	vodka martini
bourbon	rum	gin martini
canadian whiskey	bloody mary	red wine
gin	manhattan	white wine
vodka		rosé wine

Complimentary beverages are available on all
flights as announced by the flight attendant.

Catch Our Smile

Drink prices like these gave PSA passengers plenty of reasons to smile. In addition to the options listed here, coffee and beer were also offered on flights. Compare these prices to those on today's flights, where many times soft drinks are an additional charge, not to mention charges for carry-on luggage, movies, food, etc.

PSA employees were well known around California for their off-time activities through various sporting teams and events. From the early PSA women's basketball team, The Jets, to future softball teams, bike teams, ski groups, and volleyball teams, these groups helped cement the special bond that PSA employees felt towards their fellow workers. Pictured here are nearly 30 PSA employees who participated in the Tecate to Ensenada, Mexico, 75-mile bike ride in March 1979. According to *PSA Skylines Magazine*, "This was becoming an annual event with participation and crowds increasing each year."

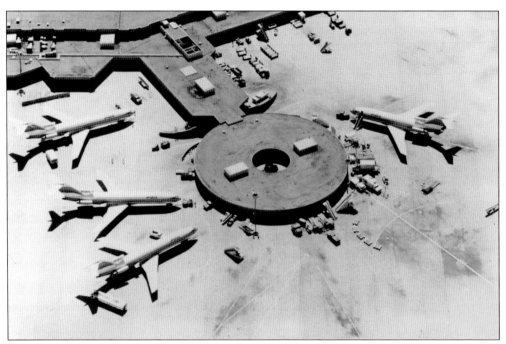

This image was taken at Lindbergh Field in the late 1970s. At this one terminal, four PSA 727s await passengers. It shows a typical busy day at the airport, where PSA was one of the most heavily utilized carriers.

Five

1980s
The Sun Sets on the Smile

As the 1970s ended, it was hard for PSA employees to imagine that the days of their company were numbered and that the scene pictured here was even possible. New rules, routes, and airplanes equaled record profits. And much of the momentum of the 1970s would carry into the new decade, as revenue and passenger numbers remained very high. New destinations were introduced, and PSA even became an international airline. In fact, it boasted in advertisements, "PSA has more flights in the West than Pan Am has in the world." PSA was now a major airline—perhaps too big. As it grew, less emphasis was put on the friendly service, which PSA became known for. Without standout customer attention or noticeably cheaper fares, PSA lost its competitive advantage. However, it would be a new trend that would be the undoing of PSA: the merging and consolidation of the airlines. Even though PSA would not survive the decade, the memories and legacy of the "World's Friendliest Airline" still live on.

smilestones

Even though PSA continued to grow, the employees strove to keep a sense of family. One way they continued to do this was with Skylines, *in which they would post important "smilestones" of PSA employees, like work anniversaries, births, and marriages.*

15 YEARS
Patricia Rosen, Res. 1-22-65

10 YEARS
Denny Gutierrez, BUR 11-11-69
Dick Jeffress, BUR 10-25-69
Jeff Davis, BUR 9-21-69
Sharon Keller, F/A 1-28-70
Teresa Pisano, F/A 1-28-70
Mary Redding, F/A 1-28-70
Kathy Schomer, F/A 1-28-70
Sharon Wing, F/A 1-28-70

Frank Araujo, AIRMO 1-4-70
Kenneth Weg, AIRMO 1-17-70

5 YEARS
Nancy Hall, F/A 1-29-75
Debra Milligan, F/A 1-29-75
Linda Muther, F/A 1-29-75
Pam Williams, F/A 1-29-75
Mary Young, F/A 1-29-75
Mary Erwin, F/A 1-18-75
Fred Coors, SJC 1-22-75

people

BIRTHS
Tana and Bob Armstrong (LAX), a daughter "Jolie Irene," 11-19-79
Gail and Dave VanSciver (Flt.), a son "Kurt David," 12-2-79
Cheryl and Marc Hansen (OAK), a daughter "Jennifer Lynn," 11-19-79
Deborah and John Brown (BUR), a son "John Paul Westly," 11-2-79
Kim and Andy Berger (BUR), a daughter "Katy L.," 11-13-79
Gloria and William T. Sommer (BUR), a son "William T. Jr.," 11-17-79
Gail and Julius Dyke (ONT), a son "Jeffrey Walter," 11-16-79

MARRIAGES
Maralyn and Joel Grimwood (BUR), 10-7-79
Susan and Jim Moore (SMF), 11-16-79
Elizabeth Mankins (SFO) and Monte Foster (SFO), 9-17-79
Lynne Ainsworth (SFO) and Glenn Young (SFO), 9-8-79

In April 1980, PSA became an international carrier by offering service from Los Angeles to the Mexican cities of Mazatlan and Puerto Vallarta; this service would last for two years. When the first PSA flight landed in Puerto Vallarta, mariachi bands and colorful dancers greeted the passengers. However, a mild recession that year did have an impact on PSA, and some California flights were cut back and service to Stockton was stopped by November.

In May 1980, PSA unveiled a new uniform for a new decade. Gone were the days of the skirt hemline above the knee. Some criticized the new uniform as representing a more conservative era in the airline.

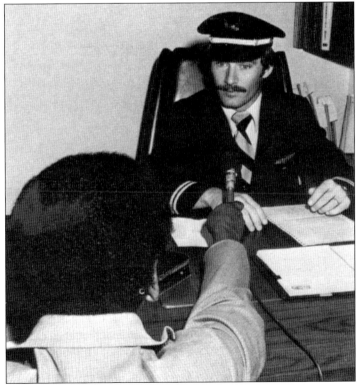

A deranged man who attempted to hijack a jet to rescue the American hostages held in Iran picked the wrong PSA captain to pull a gun on. Unknown to the gunman, pilot Alan Romantowski was a martial arts expert. After being held captive for several hours, Romantowski found his opening and knocked the gunman to the ground, disarming him.

In the summer of 1980, this smiling hot-air balloon was a common sight around San Diego. It provided excellent advertising for the airline, although on at least one occasion, it was blown far off course and had to make an emergency landing at Torrey Pines State Park.

A Douglas DC-9 Super 80, "The Smile of Burbank," is delivered to PSA in November 1980 at Long Beach, California. This was the first Super 80 to roll off the assembly line. The planes were a welcome addition to the PSA fleet with their advanced cockpit technology, excellent fuel efficiency, and quiet engines. Variants of this aircraft, redesignated MD-80s, are still in use today.

Members of the PSA family inspect a new Douglas DC-9 Super 80. The arrival of the aircraft was a welcome highlight after a period of strife. On September 25, PSA pilots initiated a strike that lasted for 52 days and grounded the airline. The strike proved to be very costly, both in terms of moral and company profits.

Soon PSA would be operating numerous DC-9 Super 80s, which replaced many of the 727s. Rather than sell the older 727s, many were leased out to other airlines or used for charter flights.

In 1981, a training center was opened at Scripps Ranch (a few miles north of San Diego) for PSA crews. The 44,000-square-foot center boasted the only DC-9 Super 80 flight simulator in the United States. The training center was much needed, as the number of PSA employees who needed to be trained swelled. By this time, the airline, which at one time operated only one DC-3, now had a fleet of over 30 aircraft, all of which utilized several flight crews in order to keep up with PSA's busy schedule.

A map that appeared in a 1981 edition of *PSA Skylines Magazine* highlights the destinations that PSA flew to. However, before the year was out, Seattle, Tucson, and Orange County would be added to PSA's schedule; it offered passengers over 1,500 flights per week in total.

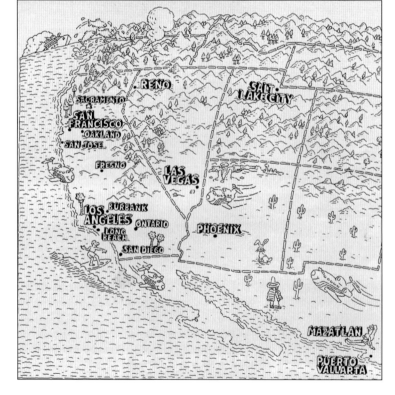

When the first PSA flight landed at John Wayne Airport in Orange County in 1981, passengers and crew were greeted by special guests. Mickey and Goofy were on hand to give out the famous mouse-ear hats complete with a PSA logo.

Throughout the history of PSA, the stewardesses and pilots received the most attention. But it took many more people to make the airline successful. Baggage handlers, gate attendants, maintenance workers, and other ground personal were essential in keeping the quick turnaround flights on time and making sure both the passengers and airplanes were smiling.

The Budweiser Clydesdale horses even made sure that passengers were happy by delivering beer directly to the airplanes. This publicity opportunity was orchestrated to announce the installation of a portable thermal storage system on the Super 80s.

In 1981, another California airline, Pacific Express, was organized to compete against PSA on many routes throughout the state. Pacific Express was at a great disadvantage, because it flew older, less fuel efficient BAC-111's, which with high fuel prices and the fierce PSA competition forced them into bankruptcy in 1984. Similar airlines, such as Sun Pacific and America West would soon be entering into the market as well.

By the 1980s, there were many airlines providing service throughout the West. As this image shows, with so much competition it became hard to distinguish PSA from the rest. In response to the crowded skies, management urged PSA employees to dedicate themselves anew to providing top-rate customer service so that the airline would shine, although some argued that not enough policies were put in place to ensure this service. In addition, PSA introduced a two-tier price structure with discount fares offered during slower travel periods.

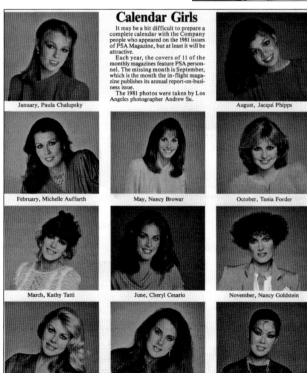

Calendar Girls

It may be a bit difficult to prepare a complete calendar with the Company people who appeared on the 1981 issues of PSA Magazine, but at least it will be attractive.

Each year, the covers of 11 of the monthly magazines feature PSA personnel. The missing month is September, which is the month the in-flight magazine publishes its annual report-on-business issue.

The 1981 photos were taken by Los Angeles photographer Andrew Su.

January, Paula Chalupsky

February, Michelle Auffarth

March, Kathy Tatti

May, Nancy Browar

June, Cheryl Cesario

August, Jacqui Phipps

October, Tania Forder

November, Nancy Goldstein

Through all of the changes, it was quite clear that one thing had not changed in the 1980s. As this photograph shows, PSA still employed many very beautiful women. However, by the start of the decade, the term "stews" or "stewardess" was being replaced by "flight attendant" in many PSA publications.

113

Valerie First is excited to hear the news that she is the 100 millionth passenger on PSA in 1981. As a result of her luck, she received a lifetime pass on any PSA flight. Unfortunately for her, the pass would only be useful for a few more years.

In 1982, a PSA legend Eleanor "Fergie" Glithero retired. Fergie started working with Friedkin Aeronautics in 1946 and had been with PSA ever since. She had served on the board of directors and held the title of treasurer and assistant secretary of PSA, Inc. During her tenure, she was credited with leading the accounting department into the computer age and developing a ticketing system that had become the fastest in the industry. But to many of her fellow employees, she was much more than this; Fergie served as a link to the past and was a walking resource about the history of the airline.

A major airline merger almost occurred in 1982, which certainly would have changed the fortunes of two carriers. In October, talks were started between PSA and Braniff International Airways about the possibility of PSA taking over the bankrupt airline's routes, aircraft, and personnel. However, the final details could not be hammered out, and the deal fell through. Braniff ended passenger service but continued as a freight operator.

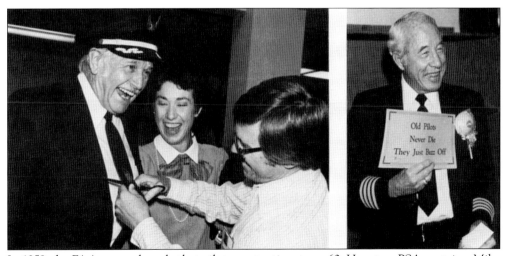

In 1959, the FAA enacted a rule that pilots must retire at age 60. Here two PSA captains, Mike Bogle (left) and Donald McDonald, celebrate their service with the airline upon reaching this milestone. The FAA has since lifted the retirement age to 65.

Flight attendant Joan Miszak slides down from a special DC-9 Super 80 tail-cone trainer at the PSA Scripps Flight Training Center. Other state-of-the-art equipment at the center were a 727 door trainer and a mock Super 80 cabin, which could simulate smoke, fire, and crash sound effects. All flight crews had to complete initial and recurring training on each type of aircraft flown, and these mock-ups allowed for the real aircraft to be used for passenger flights instead of being taken off the line for crew training.

PSA held the annual "Flight of the Eagles" in which new Eagle Scouts were flown on a PSA 727. These flights were crewed by the mini-stews of Explorer Post 727, now referred to as mini–flight attendants.

Miss Utah's float in Salt Lake City's Days of '47 parade rides on this ostentatious PSA-sponsored float. The parade celebrates the founding of the city in 1847 and served as an excellent publicity outlet for the airline, who flew to Salt Lake City.

Softball was the most popular sport at PSA. Some of these were "in-house" teams, pitting departments against each other such as the maintenance/engine overhaul team against the reservations team, or accounting against the stewardess department. Pictured here is the most improved team of 1982, the all-female slow-pitch softball team. This team represented PSA at the fourth annual McDonnell Douglas tournament in Long Beach.

Appearing in the March 1983 edition of *PSA Skylines*, this cartoon shows that the future of airline travel was very much in doubt. For PSA, this illustration would prove to be prophetic.

In the spring of 1983, PSA was able to expand into even more markets. PSA offered service to Portland, Spokane, and Albuquerque. PSA had conquered the West.

In 1983, PSA facilities at San Francisco International Airport were expanded to allow for hub operation, which allowed for easier flight connections within the PSA route system. A similar hub had already been established at Los Angeles International Airport.

The early 1980s were a time of subsidiaries for PSA. Although they were no longer in the hotel business, other profitable ventures were in operation under the banner of parent company PSA, Inc. These continued to include the Airline Training Center used to train pilots and the center's Crownair division, which sold and serviced small aircraft such as the Piper Cheyenne pictured here. The Airmotive division, which overhauled engines, and the leasing division also continued to prosper.

One of the most ambitious ventures by PSA was going into the gas business. PSA subsidiary Pacific Southwest Trading Company sold fuel to other airlines while Pacific Southwest Exploration Company specialized in energy production and exploration. In 1983, these two divisions moved their headquarters to Dallas in order to be in the middle of oil country.

In 1983, PSA became the official airline of Disneyland, and the airline started to sponsor attractions at the happiest place on earth. Here Donald Duck catches a ride on "Duck One" to celebrate his 50th anniversary. (Photograph by I. E. Quastler.)

The PSAazzers show off their stuff for the cameras. The PSAazzers were a troupe of PSA flight attendants who appeared in television commercials advertising their airline. By the 1980s, PSA commercials could be seen throughout the West Coast.

On May 11, 1984, PSA CEO Bill Shrimp (right) suddenly passed away at age 59. Paul Barkley (left), who had been the chief operating officer, was named president and CEO. He would remain in this position until the merger with US Airways in 1988. Amazingly, over the almost 40-year history of PSA, only four men would lead the company.

A PSA BAE 146-200 flies above the Golden Gate Bridge in San Francisco. The airplane, made by British Aerospace, was more fuel efficient than many of its counterparts, and PSA would operate over 20 of this type, which was first delivered to PSA in 1984. The 146 also and had short runway capability, which allowed expansion into many secondary markets. Concord and Eureka, California, Eugene and Medford, Oregon, and other small cities were added in 1985. By the end of 1985, PSA was serving 27 cities in six western states and Cabo San Lucas, Mexico.

PSA employed a simulator for the BAE to train the many crews needed for its new fleet. Although the BAE 146 was not particularly popular with pilots and passengers (due to its cramped spaces), it was a star with the accounting department because of its low operating costs. As a result, the last 727 flew for PSA in late 1984.

In 1985, an upgraded ticket machine was introduced to allow passengers quicker access to flights. This image also shows one of the new uniforms, which were becoming less and less risqué. PSA had just recently hired a marketing firm, which suggested a campaign revolving around the slogan, "We've got to be tough to make you smile." Although this campaign did reflect the difficult, competitive era of airline deregulation, to many it strayed from the basics that had made PSA successful. There was no question—times had changed.

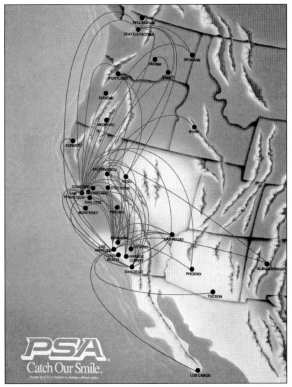

By early 1986, PSA was serving 30 cities in seven Western states, offering daily flights that, according to PSA Skylines Magazine, were more than Pan Am offered throughout the world. The fleet had grown in size to 55 aircraft with more on order, and a new marketing agreement was just signed with Northwest Airlines. There were no outward signs that PSA's days as an independent airline would be over by December of that same year.

An annual event in San Francisco is the Bay to Breakers cross-city run. PSA was represented by a mock-up of a smiling airplane carried across the city by a group of PSA employees "flying through the streets of San Francisco." As this photograph in 1986 shows, although its days were numbered, PSA employees still had a strong sense of company pride.

In 1986, American Airlines bought PSA's California rival, Air Cal. With the power of its computer reservation system and its national passenger network to feed into Air Cal, the new combined Air Cal/American was now able to fight PSA over its prized north-south commuter routes. According to *PSA Skylines Magazine*, within one hour of the American/Air Cal merger announcement, the boss of US Airways called PSA officers to propose a merger. This American 737 still has Air Cal colors. (Photograph by I. E. Quastler.)

And then in December 1986 it happened. US Airways purposed a merger with PSA, which was accepted. As planned, PSA (and the Pacific Southwest Airmotive overhaul facility) would become a subsidiary of US Airways, while the other divisions would remain independent. The CEO urged the board of directors to support the merger, pointing out that the airline had not shown a return on investment since 1979. The board agreed, and US Airways paid $17 a share for PSA airline stock. At first, it was advertised that PSA was to be an autonomous division within US Airways, with the same employees, aircraft, and livery. As this ticket envelope would indicate, it was to be more a partnership than a takeover. However, it turned out that this would be a false impression.

A terrible tragedy struck the PSA family during this time of uncertainty when on December 7, 1987, flight 1771, a BAE 146 from Los Angeles to San Francisco crashed and killed all 38 passengers and five crew members on board. An investigation revealed that a disgruntled former US Airways employee who had been transferred to work in Los Angeles for PSA, and had just been fired on suspicion of theft, caused the crash. The employee shot flight 1771's crew, causing it to lose control at 23,000 feet. All on board were killed instantly.

It soon became very clear that the merger would actually be a takeover. The PSA aircraft would now bear the US Airways livery, and all the former PSA routes would be operated under the US Airways name. During a transition period, many US Airways planes, such as this one, retained the PSA colors and smile, but soon even this would be gone. (Photograph by I. E. Quastler.)

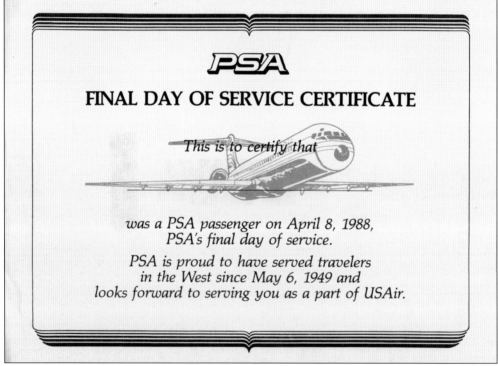

FINAL DAY OF SERVICE CERTIFICATE

This is to certify that

was a PSA passenger on April 8, 1988,
PSA's final day of service.

PSA is proud to have served travelers
in the West since May 6, 1949 and
looks forward to serving you as a part of USAir.

The last day of PSA was April 8, 1988, and the final flight that day was a BAE 146 from Los Angeles to Las Vegas. When it touched down, PSA ceased to exist. Soon US Airways would give up most of PSA's former western routes and would focus on serving the East Coast. Most PSA employees were given the option to relocate east or to take an early retirement.

Even though PSA was gone, its spirit lived on. More than 20 years have passed since the sale of PSA in 1988, and hundreds of former employees still gather each year for a picnic, to share food, trade stories, update each other on their lives, and share memories. PSA was, after all, really all about the people who worked there, not the airplanes and hangars, and that spirit lives on. It is also a tribute that former employees also maintain at least three PSA history web sites.

One of the most popular installations at the San Diego Air and Space Museum is the PSA exhibit. Hundreds of artifacts and scores of photographs, which have been donated to the museum, capture the history and spirit of the airline. The PSA stewardess uniform exhibit is one of the most commented upon at the museum, and visitors are often seen grinning as they discuss the shortness of the skirts. Even though the airline is gone, it still makes people smile!

www.arcadiapublishing.com

MAP SEARCH

Discover books about the town where you grew up, the cities where your friends and families live, the town where your parents met, or even that retirement spot you've been dreaming about. Our Web site provides history lovers with exclusive deals, advanced notification about new titles, e-mail alerts of author events, and much more.

MADE IN THE USA

Arcadia Publishing, the leading local history publisher in the United States, is committed to making history accessible and meaningful through publishing books that celebrate and preserve the heritage of America's people and places. Consistent with our mission to preserve history on a local level, this book was printed in South Carolina on American-made paper and manufactured entirely in the United States.

This book carries the accredited Forest Stewardship Council (FSC) label and is printed on 100 percent FSC-certified paper. Products carrying the FSC label are independently certified to assure consumers that they come from forests that are managed to meet the social, economic, and ecological needs of present and future generations.

FSC
Mixed Sources
Product group from well-managed forests and other controlled sources

Cert no. SW-COC-001530
www.fsc.org
© 1996 Forest Stewardship Council

Find Your Place in History.